THE SCENEBOOK
FOR ACTORS

Great Monologs & Dialogs from Contemporary & Classical Theatre

Edited by

NORMAN A. BERT

MERIWETHER PUBLISHING LTD.
Colorado Springs, Colorado

Meriwether Publishing Ltd., Publisher
PO Box 7710
Colorado Springs, CO 80933-7710

Executive editor: Arthur Zapel
Cover photography: Ted Zapel
Cover design: Thomas Myers

© Copyright MCMXC Meriwether Publishing Ltd.
Printed in the United States of America
First Edition

Library of Congress Cataloging-in-Publication Data

The Scenebook for actors : great monologs & dialogs from contemporary
    & classical theatre / edited by Norman A. Bert.
      p.   cm.
    Includes bibliographical references.
    ISBN 0-916260-65-8
    1. Monologues. 2. Dialogues. 3. Acting. I. Bert, Norman A.
PN2080.S23   1990
822'.04508--dc20
                                             90-52983
                                               CIP

5   6   7   04 05 06

For Deb Enstrom

CONTENTS

PREFACE

In selecting scenes for this book, I aimed to ensure that most of the roles would fit actors in the age range of 18 to 30. Besides the usual selection of scenes for Caucasian actors, there are a number of scenes here written specifically for African-American and Hispanic actors. The roles are fairly well balanced between male and female characters; in addition, some of the roles designated for male actors are also suitable for actresses. Samples include the Actor in Calhoun's **Audition!**, the TV Set in DeLillo's **Day Room**, the Waitress in Calhoun's **The Breakfast Special**, and even Mephistopheles in Marlowe's **Doctor Faustus**. In addition, since Amlin Gray assigns all roles — male or female — in his **How I Got That Story** to male actors, it seems reasonable that they might also all be played by actresses.

The scenes come, with few exceptions, from scripts originally written in English. Most of the source scripts were first produced since 1975, and there are also a sprinkling of scenes from classical British theatre (16th through 19th centuries). In order to facilitate scene choices, the table of contents indicates classical scenes with a *(C)* in parentheses. The book also includes a few scenes which include songs from musical theatre; these scenes are indicated in the table of contents by the symbol *(M)*.

I have attempted to assist actors who want to read the entire play from which their cutting comes by listing at least one recent publication of each of the source scripts.

Thanks to Mindi Askelson, Tabitha Bert, and Teresa Hedegaard for the research assistance they gave me. Thanks to Debra Bonogofsky for clerical assistance and for laughing with me at the vagaries of literary and dramatic agents. Thanks to Eastern Montana College's Communication Arts Department for technical support. And especially, thanks to Deb Enstrom for all of the above types of help, her constructive criticism, and her constant presence and moral support.

Norman A. Bert
Billings, Montana
1990

INTRODUCTION

Finding the Audition Monolog That Will Get You the Role

I can't even count the number of times a student actor has come to me and said, "I have this audition coming up in a couple of weeks, and I don't know what to use. Can you suggest a monolog for me?" I respond by giving the actor a scenebook like the one you are holding in your hand and wishing him/her good luck. But even as I speak I know that it's too late for this actor — at least for this audition — and that, unless everyone else trying out for that role is as poorly prepared as this actor, the role will go to someone else.

Every actor from college freshman level on up should have at least five to ten audition monologs ready to perform at a moment's notice.

Every actor from college freshman level on up should have a *growing* file of additional monologs suitable to the actor's type.

Actors without this level of preparation should be taken as seriously as an artist or designer who carries around a portfolio which contains only one picture — or maybe not even one.

So get out there, select some monologs, and prepare them.

Where will you find them?

In *play scripts.*

Of course, you can find them in scenebooks like this one. That's a lot faster. But scenes in books like this quickly become shopworn. A director who has seen fifteen Mozarts already will have a hard time staying awake for your rendition of the same speech.[1]

That means you need to read a lot of current play scripts, or classical play scripts, if you are aiming for work in a festival theatre or admission to a classical acting program. The classics are easy to find. They're there in the library just waiting for someone like you.

---

[1] *Scenebooks like this one furnish readily available material for in-class exercises, but as an actor competing for roles, you need more.*

Current scripts take a little more searching. Fireside Theatre, the drama book club, will do your looking for you at the rate of one selection a month. That's good — as a start. Address your inquiries to them at Garden City, New York 11530.

If you have local producing groups who do current plays, become a regular part of their audience.

Find out what's playing on and off Broadway and in regional theatre centers across the country, then get catalogs from Samuel French[2] and Dramatists Play Service[3] and order acting editions of plays that look interesting to you.

While you're waiting for your mailbox to fill up with the scripts you've ordered, go to the library with your copy of last week's *New York Times* theatre listings under your arm. Say hello to your fellow actor who is wading through the classics, and then check the card catalog for plays by playwrights mentioned in your copy of the *Times*. They won't be the most recent plays by these writers, but they may be something they've done in the last ten years. Don't hunt for material in anything older than that. Unless, of course, you're the one working in the classics section.

When you find a monolog that might work for you, make a note of it and start your file system. To be useful, the card ought to include the following information:

1. The names of the playwright, the play, and the character.

2. Where you found it — include the full bibliographical data for the book (author, title, publisher, and date) and where you can find the book again (Your shelves? Library [include the book's call-number]? A friend's shelves?).

3. The delineation of the cutting, meaning its act and scene location and what pages it's on.

4. A one-sentence description of the character and/or monolog to help you recall it later.

If you make it your goal to add just two cards to your file each week — even just *one* card — you will never again be in the embarrassing position of coming to me or some other acting teacher with the "what-can-I-do-for-my-audition" question. The problem is that other actors will find out about your file and start coming to *you* for advice. Sweet.

[2]*Samuel French, Inc., 45 West 25th St., New York, NY 10010.*
[3]*Dramatists Play Service, Inc., 440 Park Avenue South, New York, NY 10016.*

How do you recognize a monolog that will work? The monolog that will do the job for you needs to meet two tests: Does it fit you? And will it please the director? The second question first.

Your common sense will tell you a lot about what will work for the director. If the audition notice says "a comic monolog under two minutes in length," your three-minute Sam Shepard cutting won't do. Right? And if the company you're auditioning for is a summer stock theatre that does three musical comedies each season, your Lady Macbeth is a bad choice — just as your Evita would be wrong for your regional Shakespeare festival.

Beyond that, "what works" is pretty trendy. One year obscenities are "in"; the next year they're no-nos. One year Mamet's the magic carpet; the next he's passé. The only way to cope with this phenomenon is to attend a lot of auditions and keep your ears and eyes open. You'll find these auditions not only at local producing groups but also at state, regional, and national theatre association festivals and at the Irene Ryan Competition at your region's American College Theatre Festival. Be there and stay awake.

Audition trends may be out of your control, but at least you can pick a scene that fits you, right? Would that it were that easy!

The best audition monolog is the one that shows exactly who you are as an actor. Not what your range is, not what you *could* do if you *had* to, but what you are at center. To pick this primo monolog, it stands to reason, you need a clear perception of your type.

It's not for nothing that "Know Thyself" was writ above the Delphian Oracle, and it should be noted that, after staring at those words and listening to the oracle, most people went away none the wiser. Take Oedipus, for instance.

Student actors seem to come with charter memberships in the Oedipus club. The obvious Falstaff is fighting for the Romeo role. Brunhilda chooses an audition monolog from "Chorus Line." The actress with the sadder-but-wiser look is threatening to slash the director's tires if she doesn't get the title role in "Agnes of God." The blond hunk complains that he always gets the "heavy" role and never gets to play the romantic lead, and while he complains, you notice that his blue eyes don't melt you but instead pierce and freeze you, and you sense yourself hunting something safe to hide behind.

In class work, you may want to work at developing your breadth, playing against type, and so on, but when you go for a role, you need to know, accept, love, and project your type. You may be able to play against your type, but you can't do much to change it. But why would you want to? Your type is one of your main gifts as an actor. Make peace with your body! Make peace with yourself!

The following exercises are intended to help you in your search for your type. They are far better done in a group, since the point is to see yourself as *others* see you. Furthermore, the less the other people in the group know about "the real you," the more accurate their perceptions will be. After all, you will rarely audition for your best friend; what you want to know is how you appear to that director who's never seen you before. So get a paper and pencil, gather a group of relative strangers (not strange relatives), and begin.

First, write down five to ten things you remember people saying about you. "You're so lean." "You don't need anybody, do you?" "You have this kind of warmth about you." Things like that. If you have a hard time coming up with five, start listening to people, then go home and make notes of what they say about you.

Next, have each person in the group tell you what an obvious occupation for you would be. Hod carrier? Cocktail waitress? Accountant? Nurse? Policeman? And so on. Write down everything they say. Especially if it's news to you.

Next, have each person tell you what color you're like ("You're a vermilion person"), what kind of music you're like ("You're like a Chopin piano piece"), and what kind of animal you're like ("You're a squirrel"). Write it all down.

Have them each tell you what racial and ethnic groups you could play without make-up. Write 'em down.

What circus position would be yours? Take notes.

What kind of vegetable are you like? Write.

Have each person finish this sentence about you: "You are a (Persecutor/Victim/Rescuer). This concept comes from Eric Berne, the *Games-People-Play,* Transactional Analysis (TA) man. Write down what people say, then, if it doesn't make sense, check it out later in one of Berne's books.

Again from TA: Have each one tell you whether you seem more like a Parent (authority figure and nurturer), a Child (adventurer and rebel), or an Adult (rational decision-maker on the basis of available evidence). Make notes.

Now (probably not earlier in the sequence), have the people each tell you what roles they think you'd be great in or what actors or characters you remind them of. TV and movie roles are okay for this exercise if some in the group don't have a very broad theatre background. Write.

Now, ask each of them to write down conclusions to the following sentence starters and then give you their papers: Your primary physical trait is . . . . Your most obvious attitude toward life is . . . . Your chief emotion seems to be . . . . Your main goal in life is probably . . . . Your thinking processes seem to be characterized by . . . .

You may think of other teasers to ask. Great.

After the session, sit down in private with your notes. Pretend they are not about you but are, instead, descriptive notes about someone you've never met or a character in a play you're seeing for the first time. Make up a name for this character. Close your eyes and picture this imaginary character in a situation — something as dramatic as looking down the barrel of a rifle held by a bandit along a Mexican highway, or something as apparently innocuous as sitting at a bus stop on the bench with a beautiful stranger. Whatever. What is the character's next action? Next word? Now, eyes open again, write down the birthplace and birth date of this character. Write down something important that happened to him/her at the age of 8; the age of 15; the age of 20. Write down the major paradox in this character's life.

Then put it away. Let it ripen.

Take the whole thing out a week later, read over it, and make note of any new perspectives on yourself.

Notice that what we're looking for here is not "the real you," whatever that may be. For instance, if everything suggests you're excellent hooker material, don't go hunting a pimp — hunt roles for hooker types and quit wasting your energies on trying to become the definitive Maria Von Trapp. What you are looking for is your type, your essence as a performed character.

Now renew your search for audition pieces. Find the ones that match the profile you've discovered. They'll probably feel good. And they'll get you roles.

Developing the Audition Monolog for Performance

Question: How is the short monolog or dialog different from a full-length play?

Answer: It's shorter. That's all.

Once you understand the essential similarity between a short scene and a full play, you'll have no difficulty developing the scene for performance.

A play happens in a *place* — a geographical location complete with biomorphic or architectural details, someone's "turf." So does your monolog. Although the director may not be able to identify this location or see the details in it that your character sees, the director *will* know whether you (and your character) know — and *see* — the specified details of the place. And yes, it does matter. A lot. So design an imaginary set for your monolog, complete with colors, knickknacks, the whole banana, and then *see* and *feel* the place every time you do your scene.

A play happens in a *time* — both a chronological time specified by calendars and clocks, and also a psycho-sociological *moment* (his time, her time, the right time, the wrong time). Just as you determine and play the scene's place, discover (or invent) the scene's time and then enter that moment every time you go through it.

In a play, something is happening — there is a situation between two or more people, and through a series of events, that situation is changing. In a monolog or short scene the same thing is true; there is a situation, a set of relationships. The difference is that, due to the shortness of the monolog, probably only one event — one situation-altering occurrence — will take place. Decide for yourself, in four-part harmony, what the details of that situation are and what that event is, and each time you rehearse or perform the scene, enter into the situation fully and experience that event completely.

In a full-length play, each character has an over-all objective and encounters obstacles in his/her attempt to reach that goal. Need I repeat? Same for a scene. Again, the director may not know, from word one, what your character's motivating intention is, may not be able to name your obstacles, but the director *will* know whether *you* know and whether you are playing that intention and fighting those obstacles or whether you're just mouthing memorized words, and the director will know that *at least* as early as the first word out of your mouth, and if it's memorized words instead of an attempt to get something by the act of speaking, then you may as well save everybody's time and not begin in the first place.

A full play has a beginning, a middle, and an end. Similarly, in your monolog, something *happens* — in your character's mind, and probably around your character — to make your character start to speak. This is the beginning. Know what it is, and make it happen every time. Triggered by the beginning, your character develops what he/she has to say, fighting every moment against the obstacles which threaten to defeat his/her intentions. Finally, your character stops speaking — not because you have reached the end of the scripted text, but because something has *happened* to make your character stop speaking: Your character has experienced The End, has seen something, heard something, or felt something — either inside him/herself or outside — that has told him/her that he/she can and should stop speaking because (a) the goal has been realized, or (b) the intention has failed and should be given up, or (c) the obstacles are going to demand a regrouping or rethinking that can best be done if the character quits speaking. Experience The End every time you do your scene.

Where do you find these details of time, place, action, and character? The same place as in the case of a full-length play — by studying the text and by eking out the data you find there with research and imagination. In the case of the short scene, your text is very short — the scene itself. That, plus your imagination, is really all you need. Use the details from the "script" as the seed for developing a complete two-minute, one-person play. Or a seven-minute, two-person play.

If you have the resources, it's a good idea to read the entire play. This book lists at least one source for the full play script for each of its scenes to facilitate your task.

Reading the full script will save you time and imaginative effort in placing the scene in time, place, and situation and in inventing the many details of character you'll want to know. Furthermore, if the director asks you questions about the play, as sometimes happens, you'll look well prepared instead of lazy and ignorant.

However, reading the entire play will give you more details than you'll ever communicate in your two-minute monolog and may lead you to try to pack everything you know about the play into those few moments instead of focusing on the single task your character is trying to accomplish.

The best approach is to read the whole script, use what details you find there that will help your scene, and ignore the rest.

Enough of this. You are getting to know your type, you are hot on the trail of effective, new audition pieces, and you know what to do with them when you find them.

So get to work.

And have fun.

MONOLOGS

for Women

AGNES OF GOD

by
JOHN PIELMEIER

In this play, Dr. Livingston, a psychiatrist, has been asked to evaluate Agnes, a young nun, to determine whether or not she is competent to stand trial for murder. The murder victim was Agnes's own baby who was found in her room on the night of its birth, strangled with its umbilical cord. In addition to Agnes and the doctor, the play has one more character, Mother Miriam, the head of the convent. Agnes was physically abused by her mother when she was a child. She is naive and deeply religious; she has visions of the Lady and experiences the stigmata — that is, the wounds of Christ appear on her hands and feet. She also has a beautiful singing voice. In the process of examining Agnes, Dr. Livingston has tried to get Agnes to admit her guilt and to tell who the father was. Just prior to the present speech in Act 2, Scene 4, Agnes, under hypnosis, tells the details of killing the baby; the doctor takes her out of her trance, and, in a world of her own, Agnes continues to speak.

The first production of *Agnes of God* opened at the Actors Theatre of Louisville, Louisville, Kentucky, on March 7, 1980.

The full text of the play has been published by Nelson Doubleday, Inc., Garden City, New York. It is also available in an acting edition from Samuel French, Inc.

Scene printed by permission of author's agent, Jeannine Edmunds, Curtis Brown Ltd. Copyright © 1978, 1982.

AGNES: *(Speaking to an unseen friend)* **Why are you crying?** *(The DOCTOR and the MOTHER turn to her. Silence.)* **But *I* believe. I *do*.** *(Silence)* **Please, don't you leave me too. Oh no. Oh my God, O sweet Lady, don't leave me. Please, please don't leave me. I'll be good. I won't be your bad baby anymore.** *(She sees someone else.)* **No, Mummy. I don't want to go with you. Stop pulling me. Your hands are hot. Don't touch me like that! Oh my God, Mummy, don't burn me! *Don't burn me!*** *(Silence. She turns to MOTHER and the DOCTOR and stretches out her hands like a statue of the Lady, showing her bleeding palms. She smiles, and speaks simply and* *sanely.)* **I stood in the window of my room every night for a week. And one night I heard the most beautiful voice imaginable. It came from the middle of the wheat field beyond my room, and when I looked I saw the moon shining down on him. For six nights he sang to me. Songs I'd never heard. And on the seventh night he came to my room and opened his wings and lay on top of me. And all the while he sang.** *(Smiling and crying, she sings.)*

"Charlie's neat and Charlie's sweet,

And Charlie he's a dandy,

Every time he goes to town,

He gets his girl some candy.

Over the river and through the trees,

Over the river to Charlie's,

Over the river and through the trees,

To bake a cake for Charlie.

(MOTHER begins to take AGNES off.)

"Charlie's neat and Charlie's sweet,

And Charlie he's a dandy,

Every time he goes to town,

He get his girl some candy.

Oh, he gets his girl some candy."

THE ALCHEMIST

by
BEN JONSON

In *The Alchemist,* a good and honest man, Truewit, has abandoned London because of an epidemic and left his house in the care of his servant, Face. Face makes use of his master's absence by bringing two asssociates into the house — Dol Common, who is a prostitute and Subtle, an alchemist, who cheats people by pretending to be able to change base metals into gold. Throughout the play, this unholy trinity lures a succession of greedy, lecherous fools into their borrowed den. In the present sequence, however, from Act 1, Scene 1, their partnership is threatening to fall apart before they can profit from it. Subtle and Face have been quarreling; Subtle is holding a vial of some smelly concoction (Dol calls it his "menstrue") and Face has just drawn his sword on Subtle, threatening to turn him over to the police. Dol, however, steps in, takes charge, and in this speech forces them to patch up their differences for the good of them all.

The Alchemist was first produced in 1610.

Jonson's plays have been reprinted frequently. One recent printing is *Ben Jonson's Plays and Masques: Texts of the Plays and Masques, etc.* Robert M. Adams, ed. New York: W. W. Norton, 1979.

DOL COMMON: You'll bring your head within a coxcomb, will you?

(She snatches FACE's sword, and breaks SUBTLE's glass.)

And you, sir, with your menstrue! — Gather it up.

'Sdeath, you abominable pair of stinkards,

Leave off your barking, and grow one again,

Or, by the light that shines, I'll cut your throats.

I'll not be made a prey unto the marshal

For ne'er a snarling dog-bolt o' you both.

Ha' you together cozen'd all this while,

And all the world, and shall it now be said,

You've made most courteous shift to cozen yourselves?

(To FACE) **You will accuse him! You will "bring him in Within the statue!" Who shall take your word?**

A whoreson, upstart, apocryphal captain,
Whom not a Puritan in Blackfriars will trust
So much as for a feather! *(To SUBTLE)* And you, too,
Will give the cause, forsooth? You will insult,
And claim a primacy in the divisions?
You must be chief? As if you only had
The powder to project with, and the work
Were not begun out of equality!
The venter tripartite! All things in common!
Without priority! 'Sdeath! you perpetual curs,
Fall to your couples again, and cozen kindly,
And heartily, and lovingly, as you should,
And lose not the beginning of a term,
Or, by this hand, I shall grow factious too,
And take my part, and quit you.

THE BEAUX' STRATAGEM

by
GEORGE FARQUHAR

The Beaux' Stratagem is set in rural Litchfield, England. The beaux of the title, Aimwell and Archer, are two down-on-their-luck gentlemen who have decided to improve their fortunes by finding rich girls to marry. Aimwell quickly falls in love with Dorinda, the daughter of Lady Bountiful. Lady Bountiful, a kind, old country woman, is renowned for her ability to cure her neighbors' diseases with her home remedies, but she is foolishly fond of her son, Squire Sullen, whom the cast list describes as "a country blockhead, brutal to his wife." Mrs. Sullen finally decides to get vengeance on her husband by playing at adultery and thereby plays directly into the hands of Archer. In the present monolog from Act 2, Scene 1, Mrs. Sullen replies to Dorinda's suggestion that she has it pretty good since she shares "in all the pleasures that the country affords."

The Beaux' Stratagem was first performed at the Queen's Theatre, Haymarket, in London on March 8, 1707.

The full text of *The Beaux' Stratagem* is available in *The Complete Works of George Farquhar*, vol. 2. Charles Stonehill, ed. New York: Gordian Press, 1968 (a reprint of the Nonesuch edition of 1930), and in *Four Great Restoration Plays*. Louis B. Wright and Virginia A. LaMar, eds. New York: Washington Square Press, 1964.

MRS. SULLEN: **Country pleasures! Racks and torments! Dost think, child, that my limbs were made for leaping of ditches and clambering over stiles? or that my parents, wisely foreseeing my future happiness in country pleasures, had early instructed me in the rural accomplishments of drinking fat ale, playing at whisk, and smoking tobacco with my husband? or of spreading of plasters, brewing of diet-drinks, and stilling rosemary water with the good old gentlewoman, my mother-in-law? ... Not that I disapprove rural pleasures, as the poets have painted them; in their**

landscape, every Phyllis has her Corydon, every murmuring stream and every flow'ry mead gives fresh alarms to love. Besides, you'll find that their couples were never married. — But yonder I see my Corydon, and a sweet swain it is, Heaven knows! Come, Dorinda, don't be angry, he's my husband and your brother; and, between both, is he not a sad brute? . . . O sister, sister! if ever you marry, beware of a sullen, silent sot, one that's always musing but never thinks. There's some diversion in a talking blockhead; and since a woman must wear chains, I would have the pleasure of hearing 'em rattle a little. Now you shall see, but take this by the way. He came home this morning at his usual hour of four, wakened me out of a sweet dream of something else by tumbling over the tea table, which he broke all to pieces. After his man and he had rolled about the room, like sick passengers in a storm, he comes flounce into bed, dead as a salmon into a fishmonger's basket; his feet cold as ice, his breath hot as a furnace, and his hands and his face as greasy as his flannel nightcap. O matrimony! He tosses up the clothes with a barbarous swing over his shoulders, disorders the whole economy of my bed, leaves me half naked, and my whole night's comfort is the tuneable serenade of that wakeful nightingale, his nose! O, the pleasure of counting the melancholy clock by a snoring husband! — But now, sister, you shall see how handsomely, being a well-bred man, he will beg my pardon.

THE BEGGAR'S OPERA

by
JOHN GAY

The Beggar's Opera is set in London's underworld and its characters are thieves, thugs, professional beggars, prostitutes, and policemen. Polly, the apparently innocent daughter of a fence named Peachum, is attracted to Macheath, the leader of a gang of highwaymen. Peachum is aware of Macheath's reputation as a promiscuous lover, but more to the point, he wants a share of Macheath's wealth. He warns Polly, therefore, not to give herself to Macheath too cheaply. Polly responds to this fatherly advice with the following speech and song from Act 1, Scene 7.

The Beggar's Opera was first presented at Lincoln's Inn Fields, London, on January 29, 1728.

The full text of the play, with music, has been published by Argonaut Books of Larchmont, New York (1961), and by Baron's Educational Series of Hauppauge, New York (1962).

POLLY PEACHUM: *(As POLLY and PEACHUM enter, she is carrying a large, ornate pocket watch.)* **I know as well as any of the fine ladies how to make the most of myself and of my man too. A woman knows how to be mercenary, though she hath never been in a court or at an assembly. We have it in our natures, Papa. If I allow Captain Macheath some trifling liberties, I have this watch and other visible marks of his favor to show for it. A girl who cannot grant some things, and refuse what is most material, will make but a poor hand of her beauty, and soon be thrown upon the common.**
(She sings to the tune of a contemporary song: "What Shall I Do to Show How Much I Love Her?")
Virgins are like the fair flow'r in its lustre,
    Which in the garden enamels the ground;
Near it the bees in play flutter and cluster,
    And gaudy butterflies frolic around.

But, when once pluck'd, 'tis no longer alluring,
   To Covent-Garden 'tis sent — as yet sweet —,
There fades, and shrinks, and grows past all enduring,
   Rots, stinks, and dies, and is trod under feet.

What Shall I Do to Show How Much I Love Her?

Virgins are like the fair flow'r in its lustre, Which in the garden enamels the ground; Near it the bees in play flutter & cluster, & gaudy butterflies frolic around. But, when once pluck'd, 'tis no longer alluring, to Covent-Garden 'tis sent -- as yet sweet --, There fades, & shrinks, & grows past all enduring, Rots, stinks, & dies, & is trod under feet.

THE COUNTRY WIFE

by
WILLIAM WYCHERLEY

The Country Wife takes its title from the ingenious planning of Mr. Pinchwife: Faced with rampant adultery in London, he marries a wife from the country who, he reasons, will be naive and faithful to him. When he takes her to London, however, she quickly catches the eye of the aptly named Mr. Horner. Pinchwife decides to take his wife shopping, and in order to keep her from drawing amorous attention, he disguises her as a man whom he passes off as his wife's brother. Horner, however, sees through the disguise and manages to separate Mrs. Pinchwife from her husband and kiss her. In the present sequence from Act 4, Scene 2, Pinchwife, having discovered the event between Horner and his wife, forces her to write a letter which rejects him in no uncertain terms. The letter done, he goes out to get sealing wax and orders her to fold up the letter and write on the back, "For Mr. Horner." Mrs. Pinchwife, who enjoyed her little encounter with the stranger quite a bit more than her husband would like, is left alone just long enough to solve her problem.

The Country Wife was first performed in London in 1675.

The full text of *The Country Wife* has been edited by Steven H. Rubin and published by Chandler Publishing Company of San Francisco; it is also available in *Four Great Restoration Plays*. Louis B. Wright and Virginia A. LaMar, eds. New York: Washington Square Press, 1964.

MRS. MARGERY PINCHWIFE: **"For Mr. Horner." — So, I am glad he has told me his name. Dear Mr. Horner! But why should I send thee such a letter that will vex thee and make thee angry with me? — Well, I will not send it. — Ay, but then my husband will kill me — for I see plainly he won't let me love Mr. Horner — but what care I for my husband? I won't, so I won't, send poor Mr. Horner such a letter — But then my husband — but O, what if I writ at bottom my husband made me write it? — Ay, but then my husband would see't — Can one have no shift? Ah, a London woman would have had a hundred presently.**

Stay — what if I should write a letter, and wrap it up like this, and write upon't too? Ay, but then my husband would see't — I don't know what to do. — But yet, ivads, I'll try, so I will; for I will not send this letter to poor Mr. Horner, come what will on't.

"Dear, sweet Mr. Horner" — *(She writes and repeats what she hath writ.)* — so — "my husband would have me send you a base, rude, unmannerly letter; but I won't" — so — "and would have me forbid you loving me; but I won't" — so — "and would have me say to you I hate you, poor Mr. Horner; but I don't tell a lie for him" — there — "for I'm sure if you and I were in the country at cards together" — so — "I could not help treading on your toe under the table" — so — "or rubbing knees with you and staring in your face till you saw me" — very well — "and then looking down and blushing for an hour together" — so — "but I must make haste before my husband come: and now he has taught me to write letters, you shall have longer ones from me, who am, dear, dear, poor, dear Mr. Horner, your most humble friend and servant to command till death, — Margery Pinchwife."

Stay, I must give him a hint at bottom — so — now wrap it up just like t'other — so — now write "For Mr. Horner" — But, O, now, what shall I do with it? for here comes my husband.

THE DAY ROOM
by
DON DeLILLO

The first act of *The Day Room* takes place in a hospital room. Budge, a sixty-year-old patient has been readmitted to the hospital. Grass, his roommate, who has an intravenous apparatus attached to him, turns out to be a mental patient who wanders around the hospital. Various of the nurses and doctors also turn out to be patients from the "Arno Klein Psychiatric Wing" who are only impersonating medical personnel. In the present scene, Nurse Baker, a black woman, has just informed Budge, "We're taking you down now." Budge, terrified, protests that he's not the one they want. Nurse Baker responds with the following speech. Immediately after her last line, two masked orderlies seize her, she struggles briefly then goes limp, and they drag her out. When using the scene as a monolog, the actress may omit Grass's line near the end of the scene.

The Day Room was first presented by the American Repertory Theatre in Cambridge, Massachusetts, April, 1986.

The full text of the play has been published by Alfred A. Knopf, New York City, 1986.

NURSE BAKER: **You want desperately to believe in appearances. You want the simplest assurances. I understand completely. So many cruel deceptions. Is there anyone you can believe in? Are you talking to the person you think you're talking to? Is the person saying what you think she's saying? In this case, my case, all it takes is a glance. What is the difference, Mr. Budge, between you and me? Is it sex, or color, or age? The deepest difference is the most superficial. I'm wearing a uniform, you are not. I have authority, you do not. In all the muddle of the world, in the mixed signals, the clash, the banter, the thinking of one thing and saying of another, the saying of one thing and meaning of another, in all**

these lies and poems and civilizations, in all this razzle — it's the uniform that matters. The person in the uniform controls the facts. That's what uniforms are for. They prove that truth is possible. People who wear the same uniforms know the same things. People who wear different uniforms know different things and you can tell who knows what by the uniforms they wear. White means one thing, blue means another. You can see my authority with the naked eye. Look, right here, unmistakable, intact. *(Waits)* There's just so much time set aside for helpful explanations.

GRASS: I believe we've reached the limit.

NURSE BAKER: We're taking you down now.

THE DAY ROOM
by
DON DeLILLO

The second act of *The Day Room* takes place in a motel room which is actually the day room of the "Arno Klein Psychiatric Wing" of a hospital. For more background on this hospital, see the speeches of Nurse Baker and the TV set, together with their introductions. In the present scene, a woman and two men are eating take-out food while they wait for a group of actors to show up and perform for them. Jolene, a flamboyantly dressed and made-up black actress, enters. When she tells them nothing will happen until Klein shows up, they offer her food and ask her to talk about actors, a subject she says she hates. The woman protests that the words and speeches alone are enough to make an actor's life wonderful. Jolene responds with the following speech.

The Day Room was first presented by the American Repertory Theater in Cambridge, Massachusetts, in April, 1986.

The full text of the play has been published by Alfred A. Knopf, New York City, 1986.

From *The Day Room* by Don DeLillo. Copyright © 1986 by Don DeLillo. Reprinted by permission of Alfred A. Knopf, Inc.

Permission for readings must be secured in writing from the author's agent, Wallace and Shiel at 177 E. 70th St., New York, NY 10021.

JOLENE: I hate speeches. Look. Let me put it this way. When an athlete dies young, it's a terrible twist of nature. Something incoherent trails the event. You're left a little stunned. This boy or girl is a demon runner. Let her run. Let him jump his hurdles. It's all so innocent and swift. How different for an actor. Young, old, ancient, budding, decrepit. Dying is what we're all about. Remember the first body you ever saw, laid out, when you were little? All made-up. Rouged and waxed and clown-white. The last little slick of concealment. Well, here we are, sweetheart. We show you how to hide from what you know. There's no innocence here. Just secrets, terrors, deceptions. That's all I have to say. I've said too much. It's too damn grim. *(She takes a bite of food.)*

Look. We're just like everybody else, only quicker to pick up a danger. That's what makes an actor in the first place. That little rap of panic in the chest. We develop techniques to shield us from the facts. But they become the facts. The fear is so deep we find it waiting in the smallest role. We can't meet death on our own terms. We have no terms. Our speeches rattle in our throats. We're robbed of all consolations. Our only hope is other people. A handful, a scatter, sitting here and there, day or night — still, gray, nameless, waiting. But the parts we play in order to live make us tremble in our own skin. We're transparent. This is our mystery, our beauty, our genius, our sickness. According to Klein. *(She licks her finger.)*

We go on tonight, an hour from now, in a hospital right here in town. The psychiatric wing. There's a room called the day room. They don't use it at night. We've arranged to borrow it, transform it, do our play, disappear. Now you know.

EULOGY FOR A SMALL TIME THIEF

by
MIGUEL PIÑERO

Elaine, a teen-age prostitute, has come to a north Philadelphia apartment to meet a john. To her surprise, her "date" is her father, a middle-class businessman who doesn't know about her lifestyle. In this scene from near the end of the play, Elaine explains things to her father.

The complete play is printed in Miguel Piñero's *The Sun Always Shines for the Cool, A Midnight Moon at the Greasy Spoon, and Eulogy for a Small Time Thief.* Houston: Arte Publico Press, 1984.

ELAINE: **Look Dad, I guess it's time that we stop all this crap going on between you and me . . . First of all, you don't love or like me in the least and I can safely say that I feel the same way about you. I don't dig you at all. Maybe I'm being a little too strong on you, but that's the case. Look, I was planning on leaving you and Mom anyway to make it on my own. I don't need you anymore, and you never needed me, so I guess this takes a responsibility off your shoulders. There has never been anything for me to hold on to in that house, and I know that there never will be . . . and I don't expect . . . if after a while I stopped dreaming about it 'cause you know I always had dreams that someday you and Mom would take a few minutes off from your daily battle to offer me a sign of peace and a favor of love. I had that wonderful dream so many times that it became a rerun, stale photographs of yesterday's family album, showcasing scene in the parlor . . . life for me has begun on my terms and I am not going to give in**

an inch, not like you and her; you gave up yards until they became miles of living family nightmares. That's not for me. I lived with it sixteen years and I guess that there is nothing more brutal than that. Perhaps you will disown me. I really don't care; I enjoy being on my own. I've been saving every dime that I hustle to make my exit from that dreary existence that you call living. So drop it already, stop playing the concerned father role. It don't fit you well and it's almost making me want to throw up all over the place, so cut it loose, will ya? . . . You had your drink, now let's go before it gets too hot up here to make it out the door . . .

HELLO, BOB

by
ROBERT PATRICK

Hello, Bob is a series of short scenes in which various women converse with "Bob." Although these scenes, played one after another, create a kind of unity because of the way each woman relates to Bob, each one is complete in itself. Connie, the title character in the present scene, is a trim, direct woman in her late twenties. She wears a tailored shirt and designer blue jeans. She is at home and, immediately prior to beginning to speak, has just dialed her telephone, which has two lines.

Written for Carol Nelson, *Connie* was first performed by Ms. Nelson on April 26, 1987, at Elaine Gold's Corner Loft Studio in New York City. The longer work of which *Connie* is a part, *Hello, Bob,* is unproduced at this printing.

The complete script of *Hello, Bob* is available from the playwright, Robert Patrick, c/o La Mama, 74 A East 4th St., New York, New York 10003.

CONNIE: Hello? Samantha? This is Connie, of course. You said to call today about this time. I'm calling. Sure, I'll hold. I know how busy you must be without me there. There's my other line, anyway.

Hello? Oh, Bob. Hi. Yes, God, where have you been? Look, my boss is on the other line. Ex-boss. Hold on.

Hello? Hello? Samantha?

Bob, hi. No, I'll be on hold forever. She is the busiest woman in the world. That's why I'm so valuable to her. Did I tell you they want to fire me? That does sound sort of paradoxical, doesn't it? Wait, I'll explain. This big conglomerate took over the firm, and they want to cut my position. Say, I could care less. It means nothing to me whether I get to investigate executive expense accounts or not. Hold on.

Samantha? Are you there?

Hi, no, nothing but a tape of Burt Bacharach favorites. So where was I? Oh, yes. So Samantha says I can stay on if I'll be secretary to her and to her boss, who they're cutting his secretary, too. It's this major deal, involving passing a brand new job description, fall down and worship, at the same salary I get now. The simplest description for the proposed job would be "underpaid quarry-slave." So, I turned around and told them that I just might be talked into staying if they one: got *me* a secretary, two, gave me an office away from the parrot cage called a typing pool, and *three*, gave me my salary plus three-quarters of Samantha's boss' secretary's salary, too. Of course, it's unreasonable. I don't want to stay. Hold on.

Samantha? Testing, testing.

Bob? Huh? Oh, they're playing, "Do You Know the Way to San Jose?" So they said my new job and salary was impossible, and I told them the four-dimensional budget-juggling I'd already been doing was impossible, and they were welcome to ask that submoron accounting department to take it on *en masse*, much less find one sucker who could do it half as well as me. Hold on.

Samantha?

Bob, they're playing "What the World Needs Now Is Love, Sweet Love." I mean, look at it. Samantha, who is brilliant, took ten years to get to be a hemi-semi-demi executive, and as a woman, that's as high as she's going, so there's no chance of my advancing, so why not make impossible demands, right? And I carry her work when she has breakdowns, and I don't get breakdowns, so I must be fabulous, right? So I can always get another job, so long as there's any jobs to be gotten, however long or short that is, so what do I care anyway, right? Hold on.

Sam, for God's sake!

Bob? Before you ask, "Raindrops Keep Falling on My Head." So I draw up, on their time, a detailed description of just exactly what duties I will consider accepting, laid it on both their desks, and told the two of them that *their* current job description was to get the damned thing OK'd. And then I came home to catch up on my VCR tapes of "Days of Our Lives." I'm fed up. Hold on!

Hi, Sam? Oh, hi, Sam. Sorry to keep you waiting. Yes? Yes? Yes? Well, I would think so. You got it. Just give me forty-five minutes. Bye.

Bob? I can't talk to you now. Well, of course they did. Was there ever any doubt? Not that I care. If they'd been this sensible before, that conglomerate could never have taken over. What *are* you whistling? Wait . . . I got it: "What's It All About, Alfie?" Right? Good talking to you, too. Ciao! *(Hangs up.)*

THE LIFE AND ADVENTURES OF PERSIMMON T. HOPEWELL

by
CHRISTINE RUSCH

Persimmon T. Hopewell, a spirited, redheaded woman in her twenties, has just become engaged to Garth. To celebrate, she throws a party. She's in a festive mood and wears a pretty, peasant-style dress. The party, however, is not going as expected. The guests seem to be workmen more intent on building a deck than celebrating, and Garth seems to think Persimmon is there to audition for a play. Just prior to the following monolog from Scene 1, Persimmon has unwrapped her only present — a rope. Once the gift is open, the others ignore her and chat casually amongst themselves. Accompanied by flute and drum music from some unseen source, Persimmon begins to speak.

The Life and Adventures of Persimmon T. Hopewell is, at this printing, unproduced.

The complete script of *The Life and Adventures of Persimmon T. Hopewell* is available from the playwright, Christine Rusch, 101 Middleton Pl., Greenville, North Carolina 27858.

PERSIMMON: **Oh, no. Oh, no . . . No. I . . . I was going to be all dressed up. I thought . . . I thought you came here to see my new dress . . .** *(She demonstrates each mood, as if to hold on to it longer, as she describes them.)* **How it puffs, and clings, and swishes, and slides . . .** *(She stops abruptly.)* **Silk and . . . and cotton. Seventy-five percent . . . and . . . Garth! Oh, Garth, I would've done everything for you. Muffins and laundry and . . . It would've been . . . We could've . . . I would've . . . prayed for you . . . and . . . danced in the street just to hold you in my . . . And I'd have fought off anybody**

to protect your . . . I'd have borne you a child . . . A child, Garth, so you could . . . So you could go off and . . . So you could feel like . . . like . . . Well, you can't. It's gone. It's all gone, and you took it. *(Pause)* A love story? *(Raspberries)* There is no such thing, Garth. Do you hear me? Do you? *(Group — including GARTH — ignores her, continues to laugh, chat together.)* You don't want a beautiful girl in a pretty dress to fall in love with. And . . . and to live happily . . . ever . . . After all we planned. All we hoped for, now I know. You don't want a beautiful woman. You want . . . skin and bones and . . . and blood. You'd . . . you'd rather see a funeral than a butterfly. You prefer mermaids to wedding gowns and drunken dances to sacred rituals. But . . . but you know, you're right. You are absolutely right. All of you. So from now on, all you get from me is . . . is . . . *(PERSIMMON snatches the rope, slaps it hard against the floor. Now she sets out to reconstruct the booth. Pity whoever gets in the way.)*

THE LONDON MERCHANT

by
GEORGE LILLO

In this play, Millwood, a high-class prostitute, corrupts George Barnwell, a young apprentice merchant. Her motivation for destroying him is to avenge herself on men. First she seduces him, and then she puts him up to embezzling money from his employer, Thorowgood; finally she gets him to rob and murder his rich uncle and then turns him over to the police. In Act 4, Scene 18, from which the present speech is taken, Thorowgood and his apprentice Trueman capture Millwood and she explains the reason for her actions.

The first production of *The London Merchant, or The History of George Barnwell* opened at the Theatre-Royal in Drury Lane in London in the summer of 1731.

The full text of the play has been published by the University of Nebraska Press, Lincoln, Nebraska.

MILLWOOD: **My soul disdained, and yet disdains, dependence and contempt. Riches, no matter by what means obtained, I saw secured the worst of men from both. I found it, therefore, necessary to be rich and to that end I summoned all my arts. You call 'em wicked; be it so! They were such as my conversation with your sex had furnished me withal... Men of all degrees and all professions I have known, yet found no difference but in their several capacities. All were alike, wicked to the utmost of their power. In pride, contention, avarice, cruelty, and revenge the reverend priesthood were my unerring guides. From suburb-magistrates, who live by ruined reputations, as the unhospitable natives of Cornwall do by shipwrecks, I learned that**

to charge my innocent neighbors with my crimes was to merit their protection, for to screen the guilty is the less scandalous when many are suspected, and detraction, like darkness and death, blackens all objects and levels all distinction. Such are your venal magistrates who favor none but such as, by their office, they are sworn to punish. With them, not to be guilty is the worst of crimes and large fees, privately paid, is every needful virtue . . . I hate you all! I know you, and expect no mercy — nay, I ask for none. I have done nothing that I am sorry for. I followed my inclinations, and that the best of you does every day. All actions are alike, natural and indifferent, to man and beast who devour or are devoured as they meet with others weaker or stronger than themselves . . .

What are your laws, of which you make your boast, but the fool's wisdom and the coward's valor, the instrument and screen of all your villainies by which you punish in others what you act yourselves or would have acted, had you been in their circumstances? The judge who condemns the poor man for being a thief had been a thief himself, had he been poor. Thus, you go on deceiving and being deceived, harassing, plaguing, and destroying one another, but women are your universal prey.

Women, by whom you are, the source of joy,
With cruel arts you labor to destroy.
A thousand ways our ruin you pursue,
Yet blame in us those arts first taught by you.
Oh, may, from hence, each violated maid,
By flatt'ring, faithless, barb'rous man betray'd,
When robb'd of innocence and virgin fame,
From your destruction raise a nobler name:
To right their sex's wrongs devote their mind,
And future Millwoods prove, to plague mankind!

LOOSE ENDS

by
MICHAEL WELLER

Loose Ends traces the relationship of Paul and Susan from
their first meeting on a beach in Bali in 1970 when they are in
their early twenties until 1979 when they have been divorced.
The present monolog is from the next to the last scene in the
play, Scene 7, which takes place in 1978. Janice, Susan's long-
time friend, has come to visit, bringing along Phil, her current
man. She and Susan are sitting on Paul and Susan's terrace
soaking up the sun. She drinks a beer and smokes continuously
as she speaks. By the end of her speech, Susan has fallen asleep.
When doing the scene as a monolog, simply omit Susan's two
one-word lines at the beginning.

The original production of *Loose Ends* opened at Arena
Stage in Washington, DC, on February 2, 1979.

The full text of the play has been published by New American Library of New York City and by Nelson Doubleday, Inc.,
of Garden City, New York.

Reprinted from *Loose Ends* from *Five Plays* by Michael
Weller. Copyright © 1979, 1980, 1982 by Michael Weller. Reprinted by arrangement with New American Library, a Division
of Penguin Books USA Inc., New York, New York.

JANICE: I think it's just a question of respect. Mutual
respect.

SUSAN: Yeah.

JANICE: Phil respects me, I respect him. I mean, that's
it.

SUSAN: Yeah.

JANICE: Like with Russell, well, you never met him, but
believe me. OK, a typical example of Russell. This
time we were in Boston but you'd gone to New York
and I wanted to stop and see you; it was no big deal,
real easy to change the tickets but he wouldn't do
it. You know why? Get this. I was too attached to
the things of this world, that's what he said. OK, so
one time we were back in San Francisco and he saw

this sports car and he bought it. I couldn't believe it; he wasn't even into cars or if he was I never knew about it. I never knew a lot of things about him, but when I said what about the things of this world — I mean you can go buy a car but I can't see a friend. You know what he says? He can buy the car because he isn't attached to it, he doesn't need it. Great. And the dumb thing is I believed him. Like completely. No, not completely, no that's right, that's what I was starting to say, I really do believe there's this part of you that knows better and all it takes is for one thing to happen. Like with Russell, we were meditating one day; well, he was. I couldn't get into it so I was just sort of pretending. I did that a lot. That's another thing, I used to wonder if he knew I was pretending 'cause if he's supposed to be so spiritual he should be able to tell, right, but he never said anything. I even wondered if he knew all along but he just wasn't saying anything. Anyway, this one time I was telling you about, I just started watching him, sort of squinting, and all of a sudden he like started changing shape in front of me and I could see the pores in his skin and all these little hairs all over his body. It's like he just turned evil right in front of me. I was even thinking later that maybe it was this really ironic thing happened, you know, like the first time I finally had a mystical insight while I was meditating and what I saw was the guy that had got me into it the first time was this really evil creep. Anyway, I just got up and walked out. He was still meditating. I never saw him again. It's weird how these things work out. Oh, by the way, my mother says hi. That's another great thing about being with Phil, I can go home again. I never wanted my folks to meet Russell. Phil and Paul really seem to be hitting it off. Phil usually takes a long time to like people. It's mostly he's just shy I guess. I remember on our honeymoon we went to the Grand Canyon and he hardly talked to anyone at the hotel. I thought maybe he was angry. He's just shy. Do you like him? Sue. Susie? Susan.

THE RIVALS

by
RICHARD BRINSLEY SHERIDAN

The Rivals is set in the English resort town of Bath. Not content with true affection, the lovers in this comedy insist on intrigue and romance. The results cause them a great deal of otherwise unnecessary distress and almost lead to a duel. Just prior to the present monolog from the first scene of Act 5, Faulkland, one of the young lovers, told his beloved Julia that he must flee England because of a crime he committed; he did this to test the depth of her love — something which was never really in doubt. When she says she will become a fugitive with him, he finally believes she truly loves him. He starts to kiss her, but she fends him off and speaks as follows.

The Rivals was first performed at London's Covent Garden Theatre in 1775.

The full text of *The Rivals* is available in Richard Brinsley Sheridan's *Complete Plays,* London: Collins, 1954.

JULIA: **Hold, Faulkland! — That you are free from a crime, which I before feared to name, Heaven knows how sincerely I rejoice! These are tears of thankfulness for that! But that your cruel doubts should have urged you to an imposition that has wrung my heart, gives me now a pang more keen than I can express ...**

Yet hear me, — My father loved you, Faulkland, and you preserved the life that tender parent gave me; in his presence I pledged my hand — joyfully pledged it — where before I had given my heart. When, soon after, I lost that parent, it seemed to me that Providence had, in Faulkland, shown me whither to transfer without a pause, my grateful duty, as well as my affection; hence I have been content to bear from you what pride and delicacy would have forbid me from another. I will not upbraid you, by repeating how you have trifled with my sincerity ...

After such a year of trial, I might have flattered myself that I should not have been insulted with a new probation of my sincerity, as cruel as unnecessary! I now see it is not in your nature to be content or confident in love. With this conviction — I never will be yours. While I had hopes that my persevering attention, and unreproaching kindness, might in time reform your temper, I should have been happy to have gained a dearer influence over you; but I will not furnish you with a licensed power to keep alive an incorrigible fault, at the expense of one who never would contend with you . . .

But one word more. — As my faith has once been given to you, I never will barter it with another. — I shall pray for your happiness with the truest sincerity; and the dearest blessing I can ask of Heaven to send you will be to charm you from that unhappy temper, which alone has prevented the performance of our solemn engagement. All I request of you is that you will yourself reflect upon this infirmity, and when you number up the many true delights it has deprived you of, let it not be your least regret, that it lost you the love of one who would have followed you in beggary through the world!

'TIS PITY SHE'S A WHORE

by
JOHN FORD

Giovanni and Annabella, son and daughter of a citizen of Parma, Italy, have been lovers for almost a year, and she is pregnant with his child. She has been forced into a marriage with the corrupt nobleman, Soranzo. Soranzo, who has discovered the incestous relationship between the two, has confined Annabella to an upstairs room and has pretended to befriend Giovanni. In the present monolog from the top of the first scene of Act 5, Annabella has repented of her forbidden love and written a letter to Giovanni; she appears at her window with the letter and speaks. Actors performing the scene as a monolog may simply omit the Friar's lines.

'Tis Pity She's a Whore, first published in 1633, was performed by the Queens Servants acting company at Drury Lane Theatre in London.

The complete play was published by the University of Nebraska Press in 1966, by Hill and Wang in 1968, and by Methuen in 1975. It is also available in Havelock Ellis, ed. *John Ford: Five Plays.* New York: Hill and Wang, 1957.

ANNABELLA: **Pleasures, farewell, and all ye thriftless minutes**

Wherein false joys have spun a weary life!

To these my fortunes now I take my leave.

Thou, precious Time, that swiftly rid'st in post

Over the world, to finish-up the race

Of my last fate, here stay thy restless course,

And bear to ages that are yet unborn

A wretched, woeful woman's tragedy!

My conscience now stands up against my lust

With depositions charactered in guilt, *(Enter FRIAR below.)*

And tells me I am lost: now I confess

Beauty that clothes the outside of the face

Is cursed if it be not clothed with grace.

Here like a turtle mewed-up in a cage,

– 43 –

Unmated, I converse with air and walls,
And descant on my vile unhappiness.
O, Giovanni, thou hast had the spoil
Of thine own virtues and my modest fame,
Would thou hadst been less subject to those stars
That luckless reigned at my nativity!
O, would the scourge due to my black offense
Might pass from thee, that I alone might feel
The torment of an uncontrolled flame!

FRIAR: *(Aside)* What's this I hear?

ANNABELLA: That man, that blessed friar,
Who joined in ceremonial knot my hand
To him whose wife I now am, told me oft
I trod the path to death, and showed me how.
But they who sleep in lethargies of lust
Hug their confusion, making Heaven unjust—
And so did I.

FRIAR: *(Aside)* Here's music to the soul!

ANNABELLA: Forgive me, my good genius, and this once
Be helpful to my ends: let some good man
Pass this way, to whose trust I may commit
This paper, double-lined with tears and blood;
Which being granted, here I sadly vow
Repentance, and a leaving of that life
I long have died in.

THE TOWEL LADY

by
JANET S. TIGER

This monolog is printed here in its entirety. On stage, a
string extends from one side to the other. The woman who speaks
the monolog is of an indeterminate age — no longer young, but
not old enough to be called ancient yet.

*(A woman comes onto the stage with a basket of laundry,
which she puts down heavily. She quickly places three pairs
of men's shorts on the line, using her mouth to hold the
wooden clothespins. She is an expert at this, the way a good
sign painter is an expert at his job. Then she takes a towel
from the basket and she stops, turning to the audience,
holding the towel in a kind of reverie.)*

THE TOWEL LADY: **You know, a new towel is a wonderful
thing. Come on, you ladies all know what I'm talking
about! Now, I can understand why the men are
muttering to themselves, because no man can
appreciate a good towel. But you ladies know what
I'm saying is true! Only another woman knows what
I'm talkin' about . . .** *(She holds out the towel to
illustrate.)*

**Isn't it beautiful when it's brand new? It's so soft
and good smellin'. It has a youthful way about it,
kinda sassy, but innocent. You men are sittin' there
wonderin' why the hell you came to listen to some
old woman talk about the laundry, but if you
listened for once in your lives, maybe you'd learn
something.**

See this towel? I just bought it today. It ain't never been touched by any hands 'cept mine. Well, maybe somebody touched it in the store first, but since I didn't see it and it didn't leave no mark, it don't matter . . . *(Examining the edges)* It's perfect. I never buy those "seconds" with their funny lines down the middle and the frayed bottoms. They don't last as long. I buy one hunnert per cent thick cotton Cannon towels made for J C Penney. The thirsty ones.

Men never did understand towels. And that's because they treat their towels just like they treat their women. Here's this beautiful towel which I'll put carefully onta my towel rack. And I'll be real sure that my hands are washed clean when I use it, so's all that gets on it is water.

(She turns ornery.) But a man'll come in from working on some greasy car for three hours and he'll . . . he'll *(She can barely bring herself to say the words)* . . . he'll take those greasy, filthy hands and put them onto that clean, pure towel . . . and . . . and that towel will never be the same! No matter how I wash that towel with soap, that dirt gets right down into the fibers. And if I bleach that towel, all the newness comes right out with the grease!

And once that towel is besmirched, I dunno, it's downhill from there. But even though that towel isn't pure no more, it lasts and lasts, and that man puts more and more greasy dirt onto it, and I bleach more 'n more of the life outa it.

But just like a woman, it keeps doing what it has to do. Not complainin', just sittin' there. Until one day, there's a hole in it. Not a big one, mind ya, but it's there. When you point it out to them, they just say, *(She imitates man's voice)* "So what — lotsa good use in it."

(Back to herself) **But you can't put it out fer company no more. Naw, it gets put to the back of the closet, to be used for wipin' babies and cleanin' up after the dog.**

And then one day, *(She shudders to think about it)* **you go to get the towel to wipe up some jam that spilled onta the carpet, and . . . it's gone. You can't find it nowhere. You take all the other towels out, but there ain't hide nor hair of it.**

So you ask him, *(Sweetly)* **"Honey, did you see that towel, the one with the pretty yeller flowers on it?" And he says,** *(Imitates man's voice)* **"You mean that old faded thing with the holes in it?"**

(Back to herself) **And that's when you know the truth. You go out to the garage, and there ya see it, hangin' on a nail, just like Jesus. And it's just not mildly stained anymore, it's *covered* with disgusting marks that you don't even want to know what the origins were. And you look at that poor, faithful towel, and it's enough to make your heart just bleed!**

(She's quiet now, and holds the towel like a baby.) **And so you go inside to your husband's desk, and you take his thirty-eight, and you shoot him right through the heart.** *(A pause to let this sink in, then she is cheerful again.)*

And then you wait for the police to come and get you. *(She hangs the towel carefully, reverently, on the line. We hear a distant voice, calling from Offstage. She listens, then responds to the voice.)*

I'll be there in just a minute, Officer Williams. I just have one more thing to hang out . . .

(She takes the last shirt out of the basket and hangs it up. It has a hole in it surrounded by a big red stain. She turns to the audience and smiles, then takes the basket and walks Offstage.)

THE TRIAL OF GOD

by
ELIE WIESEL

This play takes place in 1649 during the feast of Purim in the Russian village of Shamgorod. The village has suffered a pogrom, and the only Jews left are the innkeeper and his daughter who was raped and tortured. The innkeeper decides to put God on trial for permitting the pogrom. He serves as prosecuting attorney, three wandering actors are the judges, and a cynical, diabolical stranger named Sam serves as attorney for the defense. Maria, the gentile serving woman at the inn, is thirty or less; she is tough, plump, and pretty. Just prior to the following monolog from Act 3, Sam has accused her of being immoral; he says he knows this from experience. The others question her and she admits spending a night with Sam. When they ask if he used sorcery to persuade her to give herself to him, she says he did and that she knew much happiness with him, more happiness than she had guessed existed. She pauses and then tells her story.

The full text of this play, *The Trial of God (As It Was Held on February 25, 1649 in Shamgorod)*, was published by Random House in 1979.

MARIA: Evil — is there no limit to evil? It's like pain. So much pain then, and yet some was left for now. I don't understand why . . . Walks in the field. Whispers. Silences. Timid caresses. He spoke of his love for me. He couldn't live without me. It was the first time anyone spoke to me like that. "But I've just met you," I said. Yes, but he'd seen me. Many times. From far, far away. A relative's house, a friend's farm. But — no but. I ran, he ran after me. I refused to listen, I heard nevertheless. "That's love,"

he said. It was the first time I believed it is possible
to be madly in love. Words, more words. More
meetings at night. Words — I began waiting for
them. My life was empty, empty of certain words.
His made my blood run faster. Set my mind on fire . . .
Words became caresses. I was confused. Disturbed.
Couldn't think or see. "Love," he kept on saying.
"Love justifies everything." I was afraid of the word
"everything"; also of the word "love." But — no but.
One evening I ran away from him. To my room. And
forgot to lock the door . . .

He opened it. Said he couldn't live without me.
Cried and laughed. Threatened and promised. All
the while whispering, whispering that love is more
precious than life itself . . . His hands. His face. His
lips. On me. In me. A scream. His? Mine? I thought,
Love, that's what they call love. *(Long pause. No one,
not even SAM, dares interrupt her recollection.)* **Then . . .**
the awakening. The change. He stood up and hit me
in the face. With anger. And hate. "You cheap
harlot," he shouted. "You fell for it, you really did!"
More blows and more words: which hurt more? They
kept raining on me. I was impure, unworthy because
I let him seduce me. He spat on me. What do they
call that? I wondered. I didn't know then; now I do.
Evil. That's what they call evil.

MONOLOGS

for Men

AMADEUS

by
PETER SHAFFER

This scene, from Act 2 of the play, takes place in Vienna in the late eighteenth century in the apartments of the Italian composer, Salieri. The young Mozart is with three older courtiers — Court Composer Salieri, who Mozart considers his benefactor, but who is driven by his jealousy of the young genius; Baron Van Swieten, Prefect of the Imperial Library; and Count Von Strack, Groom of the Imperial Chamber. Although most operas of the day focused on gods, kings, and heroes — like Danaius and Idomeneo in recent works by Salieri and himself — Mozart has revealed his intention to write an opera based on Beaumarchais's play, *The Marriage of Figaro,* in which servants are shown to exceed their masters in morality. The three courtiers are trying to disuade him from this project; just prior to the following monolog, they have argued that opera ennobles the listeners by celebrating the eternal through stories of the gods and heroes.

Amadeus was first performed at London's National Theatre in November, 1979. A revised version, from which this monolog is taken, was subsequently produced at the Broadhurst Theatre in New York.

The full text of the play is available in an acting edition from Samuel French, Inc., and also in a trade edition published by Harper & Row (New York) 1980, 1981.

MOZART: **If you are honest — each one of you — which of you isn't more at home with his hairdresser than Hercules? Or Horatius?** *(To SALIERI)* **Or your stupid** *Danaius,* **come to that! Or mine —** *mine! Mitradate, King of Pontus! — Idomeneo, King of Crete!* **All those anguished antiques! They're all bores! Bores, bores,**

bores! *(Suddenly he springs up and jumps on to a chair, like an orator. Declaring it.)* **All serious operas written this century are boring!** *(They turn and look at him in shocked amazement. A pause. He gives his little giggle, and then jumps up and down on the chair.)* **Look at us! Four gaping mouths. What a perfect Quartet! I'd love to write it — just this second of time, this *now*, as you are! Herr Chamberlain thinking "Impertinent Mozart: I must speak to the Emperor at once!" Herr Prefect thinking "Ignorant Mozart: debasing opera with his vulgarity!" Herr Court Composer thinking "German Mozart: what can he finally know about music?" And Herr Mozart himself, in the middle, thinking "I'm just a good fellow. Why do they all disapprove of me?"** *(Leaping off his chair. Excitedly, to VAN SWIETEN.)* **That's why opera is important, Baron. Because it's realer than any play! A dramatic poet would have to put all those thoughts down one after another to represent this second of time. The composer can put them all down at once — and still make us hear each one of them. Astonishing device: a vocal quartet!** *(More and more excited)* **... I tell you I want to write a finale lasting half an hour! A Quartet becoming a Quintet becoming a Sextet. On and on, wider and wider — all sounds multiplying and rising together — and the together making a sound entirely new! ... I bet you that's how God hears the world. Millions of sounds ascending at once and mixing in his ear to become an unending music, unimaginable to us!** *(To SALIERI.)* **That's our job! That's our job, we composers: to combine the inner minds of him and him and him, and her and her — the thoughts of chambermaids and Court Composers — and turn the audience into God.** *(Pause. SALIERI stares at him fascinated. Embarrassed, MOZART blows a raspberry and giggles.)* **I'm sorry. I talk nonsense all day: it's incurable — ask Stanzerl.** *(To VAN SWIETEN)* **My tongue is stupid. My heart isn't.**

ANGELS FALL

by
LANFORD WILSON

Angels Fall takes place at an adobe mission in northwestern New Mexico on a Saturday evening in early June. Six people have been confined to the mission's sanctuary because of a nuclear accident at a nearby uranium mine. Amongst these people are a twenty-one-year-old professional tennis player named Salvatore "Zappy" Zappala and his lover, Marion Clay, an art gallery owner in her forties. The playwright describes Zappy as "almost skinny, quite energetic." By the time the following monolog occurs in Act 2, the emergency has passed and the people are preparing to carry on with their lives. Marion has just returned from the telephone with the schedule for Zap's next tennis meet which is to be held the following day in San Diego. She tells him that his first match is at eleven in the morning with Evans, and he replies with the following lines. When performing the scene as a monolog, the actor may simply omit Marion's short speech at the beginning.

Angels Fall was commissioned and first presented by The New World Festival, Inc., in Miami, Florida, on June 19, 1982.

The full text of *Angels Fall* has been published in both paperback and hardback by Hill and Wang, New York City.

Reprinted by permission of Hill and Wang, a division of Farrar, Straus and Giroux, Inc. Excerpt from *Angels Fall* by Lanford Wilson. Copyright © 1983 by Lanford Wilson.

ZAP: Clyde Evans? *(Nod. A long pause — five seconds. Matter-of-factly.)* **That's no sweat.**

MARION: Then the winner of the Baley and Syse match. Then the winner of Bouton and Tryne or Carey and Luff. Luff is seeded eighth, believe it or not.

ZAP: *(Beat)* **Let me see.** *(She hands him her note.)* **"Zappala-Evans, Baley-Syse, Bouton-Tryne, Carey-Luff." I can take Evans in straight sets — 6-1, 6-1 if he lucks out. Baley-Syse is like a matching from the tadpole pool. Tryne gets mad, Carey is a fairy, and Luff — with all due respect to my fellow players, Luff is a cream puff. Evans, Baley, Syse, Bouton, Tryne, Carey, Luff.**

Woooo! Son-of-a — Woooo! I mean, I don't want to disparage true professionals who will, I'm sure, play up to their ability and with great heart, but this is a list of the seven most candy-ass tennis players I've ever seen. This is the Skeeter League. If I couldn't make the final eight in a — Where's Rose? Where's Charley Tick? is the question. They got all those guys together on the other leg? What kind of a lopsided draw — Tryne does not possess a serve. None. Carey is, in all humility, probably the worst professional sportsman I've ever seen. What Paul Carey most needs is vocational guidance. Syse I have personally beaten four times without him winning one game. 6-zip, 6-zip. Zap! You candy-asses. Woooo! I gotta walk, I gotta walk. You charter the plane? *(Exits)*

AUDITION

by
MATTHEW CALHOUN

This comic monolog is printed here in its entirety. Although written for a male actor, by changing a few pronouns the piece could be adapted for use by an actress.

(An actor carrying an umbrella, enters. He is anything but a leading man; perhaps he is bald, perhaps pudgy, perhaps very short, perhaps . . . something different. But not a leading man. He speaks forward to the audience, which represents the two or three people auditioning him.)

ACTOR: **My resumé.** *(He takes out a three-by-five card, and spins it forward, off the front of the stage.)* **Oh, first I should mention that I could play *any* of the parts in this play. Any. I could play an ant, I could play Little Red Riding Hood, I could play Hamlet. I've never heard of this play, as a matter of fact. It doesn't matter. I can do opera, I can do commercials, I can sing soprano, I can do my own stunts — I'm that versatile. Leading man, leading lady, gay, ingenue — you name it, I can do it. That's how great I am. I see you looking over my resumé. You're noticing I've never had a part. It's a real comment on this sick business we're in, isn't it? An actor this good** *(He thumps his chest)* **and he's blackballed! Why? *For refusing to show up at auditions!* Auditions are beneath me. I wipe my feet on them. People should be *begging* me to grace their theatres — producers should be asking *me* to audition them! But those**

egomaniacs who should bow and scrape before *me* —
they have forced me to betray my principles and
come to this *(Said with utter contempt)* **audition.** *(The
word is practically spat, or vomited out. The contempt with
which the actor feels this word is the key to this scene.)*

So no, no, don't blame *me* for demeaning myself
in this grotesque position . . . I've waited *ten years*
for them to come crawling . . . but suffice it to say
they were too wrapped up in their own insane . . .
trivium to get the hint. But enough of them. Let's
get to the situation at hand. You're sitting there
*type*casting me as a leading man, aren't you? You're
thinking that because of my matinee idol glorious
good looks, and rich, sensuous, sexy, seductive,
fetching, effervescent, tingly and charming voice, I
could *only* play a male lead. *No,* I tell you, *no!*
Observe! An ant! *(He crawls along the floor in a normal
way.)* **And now, King Lear!** *(He opens his umbrella and
pretends, in an awkward mime, to be blown around the
stage.)* **I needn't mention, of course, that that was the
fabulous storm scene, out on the heath. And now,
Brutus, impaled on his own sword!** *(Closes the
umbrella, stabs himself with it in the stomach. Dies, rather
flatly.)*

And here's a homocidal lunatic: *(He gets up, picks
up the umbrella, waves it threatening forward, like a sword.
This part seems real.)* **Give me the part or I'll *kill* you!
I'll poke out the vile grape jelly of your eyes with
the point of my umbrella! I've been waiting *ten years*
for this!** *(Puts the umbrella down.)*

**OK. All the parts. I should play *all* the parts in
your little production. Capiche? Capiche. Note the
mastery of the Spanish dialect. I do it all. Now, with
that in mind, here's my . . .** *(Abrupt pause)*

**What do you mean my time's up? I haven't done
my monolog yet!** *(Beat)* **What do you mean, next?!**

Where do you get off saying next?! I *memorized* this thing! I took the *subway* here! I elbowed my way ahead of dozens of pushy actors and still had to wait a half hour to get in here! I *wanna do my audition!*

THE BEGGAR'S OPERA

by
JOHN GAY

The Beggar's Opera is set in London's underworld and its characters are thieves, thugs, professional beggars, prostitutes, and policemen. In Act 2, Scene 4, Macheath, a swashbuckling highwayman, has called for women. A bevy of his favorite prostitutes responds to this invitation, and he greets them one by one with the following speech and song.

The Beggar's Opera was first presented at Lincoln's Inn Fields, London, on January 29, 1728.

The full text of the play, with music, has been published by Argonaut Books of Larchmont, New York (1961), and by Baron's Educational Series of Hauppauge, New York (1962).

MACHEATH: *(He greets each of the eight ladies of the evening as they enter. First through the door is MRS. COAXER.)* **Dear Mrs. Coaxer, you are welcome! You look charmingly today. I hope you don't want the repairs of quality, and lay on paint.** *(DOLLY TRULL enters as he finishes speaking to MRS. COAXER.)* **Dolly Trull! Kiss me, you slut; are you as amorous as ever, hussy? You are always so taken up with stealing hearts, that you don't allow yourself time to steal anything else. Ah, Dolly, thou wilt ever be a coquette!** *(He tears himself away from her embrace to greet MRS. VIXEN.)* **Mrs. Vixen, I'm yours. I always loved a woman of wit and spirit; they make charming mistresses, but plaguey wives.** *(As MRS. VIXEN flounces away into the room, BETTY DOXY enters.)* **Betty Doxy! Come hither, hussy. Do you drink as hard as ever? You had better stick to good wholesome beer; for in troth, Betty, strong waters will in time ruin your constitution. You should leave those to your betters.** *(She weaves her way into the room and he turns to the door to greet the queen of them all, JENNY DIVER.)* **What! And my pretty**

Jenny Diver too! As prim and demure as ever! There is not any prude, though ever so highbred, hath a more sanctified look, with a more mischievous heart. Ah! Thou art a dear, artful hypocrite. *(Next MRS. SLAMMEKIN slinks into the room.)* **Mrs. Slammekin! As careless and genteel as ever! All you fine ladies, who know your own beauty, affect an undress.** *(Enter SUKY TAWDRY.)* **But see, here's Suky Tawdry come to contradict what I was saying. Everything she gets one way, she lays out upon her back. Why, Suky, you must keep at least a dozen tally men. Molly Brazen!** *(MOLLY enters and kisses him.)* **That's well done. I love a free-hearted wench. Thou hast a most agreeable assurance, girl, and art as willing as a turtle.** *(A harp is being played in the hall outside the door.)* **But hark! I hear music. The harper is at the door. If music be the food of love, play on. E'er you seat yourselves, ladies, what think you of a dance? Come in.** *(The HARPER enters.)* **Play the French tune that Mrs. Slammekin was so fond of.**
(A dance a la ronde in the French manner ensues; near the end of it, he sings the following song to the tune "Cotillon.")
Youth's the season made for joys,
    Love is then our duty;
She alone who that employs,
    Well deserves her beauty.
Let's be gay, while we may,
    Beauty's a flower despised in decay.
Youth's the season made for joys,
    Love is then our duty.

Let us drink and sport today,
    Ours is not tomorrow.
Love with youth flies swift away,
    Age is nought but sorrow.

Dance and sing, time's on the wing,
   Life never knows the return of spring.
Let us drink and sport today,
   Ours is not tomorrow.

Cotillon

Youth's the season made for joys, Love is then our duty; She alone who that employs

Well deserves her beauty. Let's be gay, While we may, Beauty's a flower despised in decay.

Youth's the season made for joys, Love is then our duty. Let us drink and sport to-day

Ours is not to-morrow. Love with youth flies swift away, Age is nought but sorrow.

Dance and sing, Time's on the wing, Life never knows the return of spring.

Let us drink and sport today, Ours is not to-morrow.

THE CRITIC

by
RICHARD BRINSLEY SHERIDAN

This comedy is set in the London theatre world of the late eighteenth century. In the play, Mr. Dangle, an obsessive theatre fan, and his friend Mr. Sneer attend the final dress rehearsal of a new comedy by an acquaintance of theirs, Mr. Puff. Besides writing bad plays, Puff also earns a living writing for the newspapers. He specializes in writing "puffs" — advertisements which are published under the guise of being personal notices, critical reviews, or news articles. In Act 1, Scene 2, Puff claims to be the master of this kind of writing. Prodded by Dangle and Sneer to reveal the secrets of the craft, he replies with the speech presented here. When performing this cutting as a monolog, the actor may want to reassign Sneer's first line to Puff and to simply omit the interior lines of Dangle and Sneer.

The Critic, or A Tragedy Rehearsed was first performed at London's Drury Lane Theatre on October 30, 1779.

The full text of *The Critic, or A Tragedy Rehearsed* is available in Richard Brinsley Sheridan's *Complete Plays*, London: Collins, 1954.

SNEER: Well, sir, the puff preliminary?

PUFF: O, that, sir, does well in the form of a caution. In a matter of gallantry now — Sir Flimsy Gossamer wishes to be well with Lady Fanny Fete — he applies to me — I open trenches for him with a paragraph in the *Morning Post:* "It is recommended to the beautiful and accomplished Lady F four stars F dash E to be on her guard against that dangerous character, Sir F dash G; who, however pleasing and insinuating his manners may be, is certainly not remarkable for the *constancy of his attachments!*" — in italics. Here, you see, Sir Flimsy Gossamer is introduced to the particular notice of Lady Fanny, who perhaps never thought of him before — she finds herself publicly cautioned to avoid him, which naturally makes her desirous of seeing him; the observation of their acquaintance causes a pretty kind of mutual embarrassment; this produces a sort of sympathy of interest, which if Sir Flimsy is unable to improve effectually, he at least gains the credit of having their names mentioned together, by a particular set, and in a particular way — which nine times out of ten is the full accomplishment of modern gallantry.

DANGLE: Egad, Sneer, you will be quite adept in the business.

PUFF: Now, sir, the puff collateral is much used as an appendage to advertisements, and may take the form of anecdote: "Yesterday, as the celebrated George Bonmot was sauntering down St. James Street, he met the lively Lady Mary Myrtle coming out of the park. 'Good God, Lady Mary, I'm surprised to meet you in a white jacket, for I expected never to have seen you, but in a full-trimmed uniform and a light horseman's cap!' 'Heavens, George, where could you have learned that?' 'Why,' replied the wit, 'I just saw a print of you in a new publication called the *Camp Magazine* which, by-the-by, is a devilish clever thing, and is sold at Number 3, on the right hand of the way, two doors from the printing office, the corner of Ivy Lane, Paternoster Row, price only one shilling.' "

SNEER: Very ingenious indeed!

PUFF: But the puff collusive is the newest of any; for it acts in the disguise of determined hostility. It is much used by bold booksellers and enterprising poets: "An indignant correspondent observes, that the new poem called 'Beelzebub's Cotillon, or Prosperpine's Féte Champetre,' is one of the most unjustifiable performances he ever read. The severity with which certain characters are handled is quite shocking; and as there are many descriptions in it too warmly colored for female delicacy, the shameful avidity with which this piece is bought by all people of fashion is a reproach on the taste of the times, and a disgrace to the delicacy of the age." Here you see the two strongest inducements are held forth: First, that nobody ought to read it; and secondly, that everybody buys it; on the strength of which the publisher boldly prints the tenth edition, before he had sold ten of the first; and then establishes it by threatening himself with the pillory, or absolutely indicting himself for *scan. mag.*

DANGLE: Ha! Ha! Ha! 'Gad, I know it is so.

THE DAY ROOM

by
DON DeLILLO

The second act of *The Day Room* takes place in a motel room which is actually the day room of the "Arno Klein Psychiatric Wing" of a hospital. For more background on this hospital, see Nurse Baker's speech from the play and its introduction. In the room, on a wheeled swivel chair sits an extremely pale man with closely cropped hair who is wearing a straightjacket; he functions as the TV set. In the present scene, a woman named Lynette has been left alone in the room. She picks up the television's remote control device, turns on the set, and flips through the channels. As she does so, the TV set speaks the following lines.

The Day Room was first presented by the American Repertory Theater in Cambridge, Massachusetts, in April, 1986.

The full text of the play has been published by Alfred A. Knopf, New York City, 1986.

From *The Day Room* by Don DeLillo. Copyright © 1986 by Don DeLillo. Reprinted by permission of Alfred A. Knopf, Inc.

TV SET: **— except in the case of a major frontal impact, where the driver's head rockets toward the windshield at a speed exceeding —** *(Click.)*
    Promiscuous grandparents, for example. *(Click)*
    The robot's arm speaks a kind of arm language. This is the only language — *(Click)*
    There's no reason why grocery shopping can't be a shared experience. The average day is filled with opportunities for sharing. The American home can be a sharing place. Make a checklist of things you can share and keep it in a highly visible spot. A magnetic memo clipboard attached to your refrigerator or other major appliance is a good place to keep your list of shared activities. Update your list periodically. Read aloud from your list. Invent games and contests based on your list. Think

about extending your list — *(Click)*

But Mao rejected Lenin's model of revolution. *(Click)*

This is the only language the arm understands. If we want to move the robot's leg, we enter a completely different subroutine. *(Click)*

It affects me. It affects my husband. It affects — *(Click)*

Nytex, Westlab, Telcon, Syntech, Microdyne. *(Click)*

We're talking pound after pound after pound. *(Click)*

Lackluster industrials. *(Click)*

Irreversible comas. *(Click)*

Saturated fats. *(Click)*

But Betty never suspected that the bottle with the blue detergent — *(Click)*

Now hold the paper and get ready to make your *h*. Put your pencil on the baseline and make your *h* to the numerical count of seven. Here we go. Undercurve, loop, slant, pause, retrace, overcurve, slant. Look at your *h*. Look at my *h*. We can use the letter *h* in the word "horse." Here is the word "horse." You all know what a horse looks like. This is what the word looks like. Is there anyone who sees a resemblance? *(A knock on the door. LYNETTE turns off the TV.)*

FAMILY VOICES

by
HAROLD PINTER

The monolog printed here is the first in a series of state-
ments made by three family members — Voice 1, the son, Voice
2, his mother, and Voice 3, his dead father. Voice 1 always
addresses his comments to his mother; Voices 2 and 3 always
address their son. Throughout the play, the mother frequently
blames her son for never writing to her, the father says he wants
to communicate with the son but can't because he's dead, and
the son tells about finding a new family for himself in the house
of Mrs. Withers.

Family Voices is one of three plays united under the title
Other Places. The other two plays in the Tryptich are *Victoria
Station* and *A Kind of Alaska. Other Places* was first performed
in the Cottesloe auditorium of the National Theatre, London,
on October 14, 1982. *Family Voices* was first broadcast on BBC
Radio 3 on January 22, 1981.

The play is printed in full in Harold Pinter's *Other Places:
Three Plays,* New York: Grove Press, 1982.

This scene from *Family Voices* is reprinted by permission
of Grove Press, a division of Wheatland Corporation. Copyright
© 1981, 1982.

VOICE 1:   I am having a very nice time.

**The weather is up and down, but surprisingly
warm, on the whole, more often than not.**

**I hope you're feeling well, and not as peaky as
you did the last time I saw you.**

**No, you didn't feel peaky, you felt perfectly well,
you simply looked peaky.**

Do you miss me?

**I am having a very nice time and I hope you are
glad of that.**

At the moment I am dead drunk.

**I had five pints in The Fishmongers Arms tonight,
followed by three double scotches, and literally
rolled home.**

When I say home I can assure you that my room is extremely pleasant. So is the bathroom. Extremely pleasant. I have some very pleasant baths indeed in the bathroom. So does everybody else in the house. They all lie quite naked in the bath and have very pleasant baths indeed. All the people in the house go about saying what a superb bath and bathroom the one we share is. They go about telling literally everyone they meet what lovely baths you can get in this place, more or less unparalleled, to put it bluntly.

It's got a lot to do with the landlady, who is a Mrs. Withers, a person who turns out to be an utterly charming person of impeccable credentials.

When I said I was drunk I was of course making a joke.

I bet you laughed.

Mother?

Did you get the joke? You know I never touch alcohol.

I like being in this enormous city all by myself. I expect to make friends in the not too distant future.

I expect to make girlfriends too.

I expect to meet a very nice girl. Having met her, I shall bring her home to meet my mother.

I like walking in this enormous city all by myself. It's fun to know no one at all. When I pass people in the street they don't realize that I don't know them from Adam. They know other people and even more other people know them, so they naturally think that even if I don't know them I know the other people. So they look at me, they try to catch my eye, they expect me to speak. But as I do not know them I do not speak. Nor do I ever feel the slightest temptation to do so.

You see, Mother, I am not lonely because all that has ever happened to me is with me, keeps me company; my childhood, for example, through which you, my mother, and he, my father, guided me.

I get on very well with my landlady, Mrs. Withers. She

tells me I am her solace. I have a drink with her at lunch time and another one at tea time and then take her for a couple in the evening at The Fishmongers Arms.

She was in the Women's Air Force in the Second World War. "Don't drop a bollock, Charlie," she's fond of saying. "Call him Flight Sergeant and he'll be happy as a pig in shit."

You'd really like her, Mother.

I think it's dawn. I can see it coming up. Another day. A day I warmly welcome. And so I shall end this letter to you, my dear mother, with my love.

FIVE IN THE KILLING ZONE

by
LAVONNE MUELLER

This play focuses on a five-man medical unit in a free-fire zone in Vietnam; the set is a bombed-out pagoda which they have turned into a field laboratory. The unit's mission is to identify the remains of dead soldiers; their goal is to find one set of remains which they can't identify and which can, therefore, qualify for the unknown soldier of the Vietnam War. The commanding officer of the unit is Captain Odom, a black man who went through West Point. He is efficient and motivated, a careful scientist, a strict disciplinarian who is also concerned about the well-being of his men and the dignity of the shards of human flesh they work with. He has let everyone believe he's a medical doctor until moments before this speech from Act 2 when the men confront him demanding to know the truth, and his suppressed rage explodes. He rolls up his sleeves to reveal arms that are pock-marked and permanently bruised, and begins to speak.

Five in the Killing Zone was first done as a workshop by the Women's Project at New York City's American Place Theatre in March, 1985. The play won a Drama League Award and a New York Foundation for the Arts Fellowship.

In 1989, the complete script of *Five in the Killing Zone* was published by Applause Books, New York City, in the anthology *Womenswork*.

ODOM: You ask me . . . am I a *real* doctor? *(Pause)* **You don't have a chance, the dean told me. Medical school's . . . restricted. There's a tight quota. It's controlled. Regulated. It's . . . exclusive.** *(Pause)*

Go into veterinary medicine, my West Point CO told me. The quota's more lax there . . . more . . . accessible . . . for people like you. And you get the

same kind of training. You're a doctor in the end. *(Pause)*

Look, boy, we gave you the Point. You can't have everything. *(Pause)*

There are more civilized ways to get a black man. West Point officer ways. *(Pause)*

My official shots record kept getting lost. I had to undergo the full battery of inoculations . . . over and over . . . till my arms ended up looking like this. *(Pause)*

Let me tell you something, every black man listening. It will get you through prep school. It will get you through West Point. It will get you through life. *(Pause)*

When you get up in the morning and look at yourself in the mirror, make sure you see nothing. Make sure what's looking back at you is an empty face. Empty. Like the mask the Aztec dead wear. A mask that doesn't haunt the living. *(Pause)*

Put your shirt on every morning, sleeve by sleeve. Keep inside yourself like a hidden friend. There's a trick to the lips dreaming. *(Pause)*

Live the days . . . here! *(Hits his chest.)*

Days that come unknown with secret hands. *(Pause)*

It doesn't take long to find you're just an ugly blackbird — a hundred dreams a year like feathers falling off — that won't grow back. *(Pause)*

Yes. I'm a veterinarian.

GEMINI

by
ALBERT INNAURATO

The action of *Gemini* takes place in the Italian section of South Philadelphia in early summer, 1973. The play occurs when Francis Geminiani, a Harvard student, comes home to celebrate his twenty-first birthday. Herschel Weinberger lives next door to the Geminiani family with his mother, a rough-talking, hard-drinking, blowsy woman of forty. According to the play's character description, Herschel "is sixteen, very heavy, asthmatic, very bright, but eccentric. He is obsessed with Public Transportation in all its manifestations, and is shy and a little backward socially." In this cutting from Act 1, Scene 2, Herschel is talking to Judith, Francis's exceedingly beautiful girlfriend. Randy, mentioned by Herschel, is Judith's nineteen-year-old brother. Just before Herschel begins to speak, Judith has asked, "Why are you so interested in the subways?"

Gemini was first performed at New York City's Little Theatre on May 21, 1977. Albert Innaurato received an Obie for distinguished playwriting for *Gemini*.

The play is printed in full in *Two Plays by Albert Innaurato: Gemini and The Transfiguration of Benno Blimpie*. Clifton, New Jersey: James T. White, 1977.

This scene from *Gemini* is reprinted by permission of the author. Copyright © 1978 Albert Innaurato.

HERSCHEL: Oh, not just the subways. I love buses too, you know? And my favorites are, well, you won't laugh? The trolleys. They are very beautiful. There's a trolley graveyard about two blocks from here. I was thinking, like maybe Randy would like to see that, you know? I could go see the engine any time. The trolley graveyard is well, like, I guess, beautiful, you know? Really. They're just there, like old creatures everyone's forgotten, some of them rusted out, and some of them on their sides, and one, the old thirty-two, is like standing straight up as though sayin', like, I'm going to stand here and be myself, no matter what. I talk to them. Oh, I shouldn't have said that. Don't tell my mother, please. It's, you know, like people who go to castles and look for, for, well, like, knights in shining armor, you know? That past was beautiful and somehow, like, pure. The same is true of the trolleys. I follow the old thirty-two route all the time. It leads right to the graveyard where the thirty-two is buried, you know? It's like, well, fate. The tracks are half-covered with filth and pitch, new pitch like the city pours on. It oozes in the summer and people walk on it, but you can see the tracks and you see, like, it's true, like, old things last, good things last, like, you know? The trolleys are all filthy and half-covered and rusted out and laughed at, and even though they're not much use to anybody and kind of ugly like, by most standards, they're, like, they're, well, I guess, beautiful, you know?

HOW I GOT THAT STORY

by
AMLIN GRAY

This play takes place in a southeast Asian country called Am-Bo Land where the USA is helping the government in its war against guerrilla insurgents. The play has only two actors; one plays the Reporter, who is in his late twenties, and the other plays all the other roles, including Americans and Ambonese, men and women, young people and old. In the play's first scene, titled "Accreditation," the Reporter goes to get his credentials from the Am-Bo Land offices of the firm which has hired him, TransPanGlobal Wire Service. In the present monolog, Kingsley, one of the firm's managers, informs him about reportorial realities in Am-Bo Land. Actors performing the scene as a monolog may simply omit the reporter's lines.

How I Got That Story was first performed by the Milwaukee Repertory Theater on April 12, 1979.

The full text of the play is available in an acting edition from Dramatists Play Service, Inc. It has also been published by Nelson Doubleday (Garden City, New York) and also in James Reston, Jr., ed. *Coming to Terms: American Plays & the Vietnam War.* New York: Theatre Communications Group, 1985.

KINGSLEY: To bring this down to cases. The government of Madame Ing is fighting for its life. You probably know that the guerrillas don't confine themselves to Robert's Rules of Order. Madame Ing is forced, in kind, to bite and scratch a little. You may see a few examples. Some abridgement of the freedom of internal opposition. Some abridgement of the outer

– 79 –

limbs of those involved. These things may rock you.
Nothing wrong with that — as long as you keep one
thing very firmly in mind. When we send out reports,
the nearest terminal for them is the Imperial Palace.
Madame Ing eats ticker tape like eel in fish sauce.
That's the A-1 delicacy here, you'll have to try it. Can
you handle chopsticks?

REPORTER: Yes, I —

KINGSLEY: Madame Ing is very sensitive to how she's
viewed from overseas. Let's face it. When we applied
for permission to set up an agency here, we didn't
apply to the guerrillas. It's Ing who allowed us to
come here, and it's Ing who has the power to send
us back. *(Sliding a card across the desk to the
REPORTER.)* Let's have a signature.

REPORTER: What's this?

KINGSLEY: Your press card.

REPORTER: *(Pleased)* Oh. *(He signs.)*

KINGSLEY: *(Deftly seals the card in plastic)* You'll find this
plastic proof against the rainy season, jungle rot. I
took a card like this intact right off the body of a
newsman who had all but decomposed.

REPORTER: What happened to him?

KINGSLEY: Madame Ing expelled him but he didn't
leave. The will of a developing government will find
a way. *(He hands the REPORTER his sealed card.)* We're
very glad you're with us.

LOOSE ENDS

by
MICHAEL WELLER

Loose Ends traces the relationship of Paul and Susan from their first meeting on a beach on Bali in 1970 when they are in their early twenties until 1979 when they have been divorced. The present monolog is from Scene 4 which takes place in 1974 when Paul and Susan have been living together for about three years. Susan has gone to New York on a business trip — their first time apart since they've been living together. Selina, Paul's co-writer, is at his house to work on a film script with him. He's nervous because Susan wasn't at her hotel room when he called the previous evening. Selina asks if he thinks she was out with another man and goes on to say that, if she was in love with a man and he did that to her, she'd kill him. The following speech is Paul's reply. When doing the scene as a monolog, omit Selina's internal line.

The original production of *Loose Ends* opened at Arena Stage in Washington, DC, on February 2, 1979.

The full text of the play has been published by New American Library of New York City and by Nelson Doubleday, Inc., of Garden City, New York.

PAUL: We've always had this kind of an understanding, not like a formal thing, just we picked it up talking to each other that it'd be all right if we . . . in theory, that is, in theory it was OK if we, we weren't like exclusively tied down to each other, you know, if we were attracted to someone . . . and we didn't have to necessarily tell each other if we ever, unless we were afraid it was getting out of hand, like it was getting too serious and we couldn't handle it. But the thing is, we've never been unfaithful. Unfaithful. Funny how it comes back to words like that. We haven't slept with other people. At least I haven't.

And I don't think she has, except of course, there's no way to know for sure since we said we didn't necessarily have to tell each other, but I really don't think she has. She's probably wanted to. I mean I've wanted to, so it stands to reason that she's probably wanted to and the fact that she hasn't, or probably hasn't, uncool though it is to admit it, the fact that there's probably this thing she's wanted to do but didn't do it because she knew how it'd make me feel ... that always made me feel, like, admire her. Not admire exactly. Maybe trust. Respect. Trust. Something like that. Some combination of those things.

SELINA: I know what you mean.

PAUL: Yeah, but now that I don't know where she was last night I've been feeling pretty ridiculous, you know. Kind of foolish. Stupid, I don't know what. I was awake all last night thinking about it. I mean, here I am all this time, I've known you for what, two years, and all that time I've found you like very, very attractive, but so what, that's how it goes and now if she's just gone and slept with someone, what was all this about? All this holding back for the sake of someone else's feelings and the most ridiculous thing of all is maybe she was in New York thinking you and me were getting it on behind her back and that's what made her ... if in fact she did do anything, maybe she did it to get even. Or maybe she hasn't done anything. In which case where was she? And why didn't she call?

MA RAINEY'S BLACK BOTTOM

by
AUGUST WILSON

Ma Rainey's Black Bottom takes place in a Chicago recording studio in early March, 1927, where white producers are making a recording of black jazz star Ma Rainey. In the present scene from the end of Act 1, the back-up group is rehearsing. The group consists of several black musicians in their fifties and Levee, a trumpet player in his early thirties. Levee has his own introduction to one of the pieces and is arguing with the older musicians. When the white technician, Sturdyvant, breaks in to get them to stop arguing and Levee responds, "Yessir," the other musicians say he's "spooked up with the white man." The following monolog is Levee's response.

Ma Rainey's Black Bottom opened at the Yale Repertory Theater, New Haven, Connecticut on April 6, 1984.

The full text of the play was published by New American Library, New York, in 1985.

LEVEE: Levee got to be Levee! And he don't need nobody messing with him about the white man — 'cause you don't know nothing about me. You don't know Levee. You don't know nothing about what kind of blood I got! What kind of heart I got beating here! *(He pounds his chest.)*

I was eight years old when I watched a gang of white mens come into my daddy's house and have to do with my mama any way they wanted. *(Pauses)*

We was living in Jefferson County, about eighty miles outside of Natchez. My daddy's name was Memphis ... Memphis Lee Green ... had him near fifty acres of good farming land. I'm talking about good land! Grow anything you want! He done gone off of shares and bought this land from Mr. Hallie's widow woman after he done passed on. Folks called him an uppity nigger 'cause he done saved and borrowed to where he could buy this land and be independent. *(Pauses)*

It was coming on planting time and my daddy went into Natchez to get him some seed and fertilizer. Called me, say, "Levee, you the man of the house now. Take care of your mama while I'm gone." I wasn't but a little boy, eight years old. *(Pauses)*

My mama was frying up some chicken when them mens come in that house. Must have been eight or nine of them. She standing there frying that chicken and them mens come and took hold of her just like you take hold of a mule and make him do what you want. *(Pauses)*

There was my mama with a gang of white mens. She tried to fight them off, but I could see where it wasn't gonna do her any good. I didn't know what they were doing to her . . . but I figured whatever it was they may as well do to me too. My daddy had a knife that he kept around there for hunting and working and whatnot. I knew where he kept it and I went and got it.

I'm gonna show you how spooked up I was by the white man. I tried my damndest to cut one of them's throat! I hit him on the shoulder with it. He reached back and grabbed hold of that knife and whacked me across the chest with it. *(LEVEE raises his shirt to show a long ugly scar.)* That's what made them stop. They was scared I was gonna bleed to death. My mama wrapped a sheet around me and carried me two miles down to the Furlow place and they drove me up to Doc Albans. He was waiting on a calf to be born, and say he ain't got time to see me. They carried me up to Miss Etta, the midwife, and she fixed me up.

My daddy came back and acted like he done accepted the facts of what happened. But he got the names of them mens from Mama. He found out who they was and then we announced we was moving out of that county. Said good-by to everybody . . . all the neighbors. My daddy went and smiled in the face of one of them crackers who had been with my mama. Smiled in his face and sold him our land. We moved over with relations in Caldwell. He got us settled in and then he took off one day. I ain't never seen him since. He sneaked back, hiding up in the woods, laying to get them eight or nine men. *(Pauses)*

He got four of them before they got him. They tracked him down in the woods. Caught up with him and hung him and set him afire. *(Pauses)*

My daddy wasn't spooked up by the white man. Nosir! And that taught me how to handle them. I seen my daddy go up and grin in this cracker's face . . . smile in his face and sell him his land. All the while he's planning how he's gonna get him and what he's gonna do to him. That taught me how to handle them. So you all just back up and leave Levee alone about the white man. I can smile and say yessir to whoever I please. I got time coming to me. You all just leave Levee alone about the white man.

MUGGINS

by
CHRISTINE RUSCH

Muggins is about Mary Lou, a woman who has just discovered that her husband Paul has been seeing her best friend Darcy. Mary Lou sets up a dinner party to punish Darcy, but she succeeds only in hurting her dear friend Wade. Although far more interesting than meat-and-potatoes Paul, Wade is gay. When he sees what is really going on, Wade tries to take control; he stands up and finally speaks the words he has always wanted Mary Lou to hear — the present speech. In the end, Wade recovers and everyone has breakfast together.

Muggins was first performed by the Playwrights' Forum at the Mint Museum of Art's Golden Circle Theatre in Charlotte, North Carolina, in January, 1983.

The complete script of *Muggins* is available from the playwright, Christine Rusch, 101 Middleton Place, Greenville, North Carolina 27858.

WADE: Nobody respects chickens, Mary Lou. Blue jays, maybe, or snowy headed egrets . . . but not chickens. You go in there eggin', wet feathers still stickin', grab them from their mama, laugh when she cries. It's all she can do, Mary Lou. Boil 'em, fry 'em, poach 'em, scramble 'em, stuff 'em, use what they're made of . . . to thicken, glaze, hold together what's meant to be apart. Color 'em, yeah, color 'em: Little pink and white corpses stuck in baskets to celebrate . . . Spring time. You call that respect? You ever found one? Broke open your four-minute special and there's a heat-frozen beginning . . . ended? A carcass, like a roach in an oatmeal cookie, except the roach don't belong. The baby chick, now, that egg's his place. And you break it open and there he is, and you push it away and you grab your toast. The babies we don't steal get to grow. They grow the way we tell them to grow, with tender legs, big breasts, and easy-pull pin feathers. And when they're the best they can be . . . we chop off their heads. Because everybody scarfs chickens, Mary Lou. We repay them with insults: Chicken-hearted, chicken-livered, chicken, like don't be chicken. But we are, more than we'd say. We can't do without them, that's why. And you know it. And I know it. Chicken shit. So we hate them. With a special hate we save for what we need. I think they know. Some of them show it, if you look really close . . . chickens got feelings, Mary Lou. But . . . But they don't get no respect.

STREAMERS
by
DAVID RABE

Streamers takes place in the mid 1960s in the cadre room of an army barracks in Virginia. Throughout the beginning of the play, one of the young soldiers who lives there, Richie, has been making passes at another one, Billy. No one is sure whether Richie is serious or not, but his constant gay innuendoes have everyone tense. In the present scene, Richie, Billy, and their black roommate Roger are in their beds after the lights have gone out. Billy tells the following story to explain his feelings about homosexuality.

Streamers was first presented at the Long Wharf Theatre in New Haven, Connecticut, in January, 1976. It won the New York Drama Critics Circle Award as the best American play of 1976.

The full text of the play was published by Alfred A. Knopf, New York City, in 1977. It was also published in James Reston, Jr., ed. *Coming to Terms: American Plays & the Vietnam War.* New York: Theatre Communications Group, 1985.

BILLY: I ... had a buddy, Rog — and this is the whole thing, this is the whole point — a kid I grew up with, played ball with in high school, and he was a tough little cat, a real bad man sometimes. Used to have gangster pictures up in his room. Anyway, we got into this deal where we'd drive on down to the big city, man, you know, hit the bad spots, let some queer pick us up ... sort of ... long enough to buy us some good stuff. It was kinda the thing to do for a while, and we all did it, the whole gang of us. So we'd let these cats pick us up, most of 'em old guys, and they were hurtin' and happy as hell to have us, and we'd get a lot of free booze, maybe a meal, and we'd turn 'em on. Then pretty soon they'd ask us did we want

to go over to their place. Sure, we'd say, and order one more drink, and then when we hit the street, we'd tell 'em to kiss off. We'd call 'em fag and queer and jazz like that and tell 'em to kiss off. And Frankie, the kid I'm tellin' you about, he had a mean streak in him and if they gave us a bad time at all, he'd put 'em down. That's the way he was. So that kinda jazz went on and on for sort of a long time and it was a good deal if we were low on cash or needed a laugh and it went on for a while. And then Frankie — one day he come up to me — and he says he was goin' home with the guy he was with. He said, what the hell, what did it matter? And he's sayin' — Frankie's sayin' — why don't I tag along? What the hell, he's sayin', what does it matter who does it to you, some broad or some old guy, you close your eyes, a mouth's a mouth, it don't matter — that's what he's sayin'. I tried to talk him out of it, but he wasn't hearin' anything I was sayin'. So the next day, see, he calls me up to tell me about it. OK, OK, he says, it was a cool scene, he says; they played poker, a buck minimum, and he made a fortune. Frankie was eatin' it up, man. It was a pretty way to live, he says. So he stayed at it, and he had this nice little girl he was goin' with at the time. You know the way a real bad cat can sometimes do that — have a good little girl who's crazy about him and he is for her, too, and he's a different cat when he's with her? . . .

Well, that was him and Linda, and then one day he dropped her, he cut her loose. He was hooked, man. He was into it, with no way he knew out — you understand what I'm sayin'? He had got his ass hooked. He had never thought he would and then one day he woke up and he was on it. He just hadn't been told, that's the way I figure it; somebody didn't

tell him somethin' he shoulda been told and he come
to me wailin' one day, man, all broke up and wailin',
my boy Frankie, my main man, and he was a fag. He
was a faggot, black Roger, and I'm not lyin'. I am
not lyin' to you.

THE SUN ALWAYS SHINES
FOR THE COOL

by
MIGUEL PIÑERO

In this scene from near the end of the play's first act, the young pimp, Cat Eyes, is talking to an older man, Viejo. It's near midnight in a big-city bar frequented by hustlers, hookers, and other "players of the city." According to the introductory stage direction, all the people in the bar are extremely well-dressed. Bam-Bam and Satisfaction, who enter toward the end of the scene, are prostitutes. Although Cat Eyes doesn't know it, Chile, the girl he says he *plans* to turn into a prostitute, is Viejo's daughter. When using this scene as a monolog, the actor may omit Viejo's two speeches.

The complete play is printed in Miguel Piñero's *The Sun Always Shines for the Cool, A Midnight Moon at the Greasy Spoon, and Eulogy for a Small Time Thief.* Houston: Arte Publico Press, 1984.

This scene from *The Sun Always Shines for the Cool* is reprinted by permission of Arte Publico Press. Copyright © Miguel Piñero 1984.

CAT EYES: You see them dudes? They think they got it made.

VIEJO: Don't you?

CAT EYES: They got some of it made, but not all of it. They got themselves years ahead of me in the game ... plenty of time in the life to learn much experience. But me, I came fast, Viejo, faster than any of them. That's why they don't like me, cuz they all know that I'm swifter than any of them were at my age, man. I am a young blood fresh off the doctor's mitts. You know I still have the smell of the afterbirth hanging about me ... but I'm swifter than those people who call themselves "folks," and have the smell of death in the breath. Me? I am new life, Viejo, I am new life. You think I don't know they are jealous of me and my fast-talking self. Man. I know that. Shit, that is why I talk to them the way I do cuz I know that. You think I may be wrong, but I'm not ... I'm not ... Viejo, my rap is strong and my words are never wrong. I'm young and faster than a streak of lightning and a ball of heat ... and I always land on my feet ... ever since I could remember I never touched the floor with my knees. You see that girl, Chile; they all wanted her but they all fear Justice and Lefty Gorilla, but not me cuz their time is up on the earth. I know that his is a jungle law ... *(Enter BAM-BAM and SATISFACTION)* and I'm staking my name to that game. She is gonna make me a very wealthy man, my man. She is gonna put me on the mack map of the year ... every year until doomsday.

VIEJO: Are you saying what I think you are saying?

CAT EYES: That's right, mister. I'm gonna turn her sweet ass out.

TRANSFUSION

by
JANET S. TIGER

Transfusion takes place in a small midwestern town. By the beginning of Act 2, Scene 2, when the following monolog occurs, John Sanderson, a redneck laborer in his fifties, has learned he is dying of AIDS. He contracted the disease four years earlier, in 1976, during an operation for cancer, when he received a blood transfusion from his gay son who is also now dying of AIDS. John is wearing a bathrobe which has become too large for him; he has a deep, hidden anger. He delivers the speech directly to the audience.

Transfusion was first produced at the Gaslamp Quarter Theatre in San Diego, California in February, 1988.

The complete script is available from the playwright, Janet S. Tiger, 4489 Bertha St., San Diego, California 92117.

JOHN: **I have never liked the sight of blood. When I was a boy, I hated when I cut myself. I didn't like fighting because I didn't like bleeding — mine or theirs. My wife used to say that it was a good thing I wasn't born female, because I never would have lasted through menstruation.**

I was one of those guys who fainted when they took the blood sample during Army induction. During the war, they gave me the Purple Heart, but I never tell people because I never felt I really deserved it.

You see, I was in a ditch, right next to my buddy Louis. Louis was from New York, a little guy, always making jokes. One minute he was there, laughing, and the next, a shell hit. When I looked over to see if

he was all right, he was gone. There was just a pile of flesh covered with blood. I fainted.

When I woke up, I was in the hospital. The medics had found me unconscious, covered with blood, and thought I was wounded too. I was delirious for a while, and they didn't listen when I said it was all a mistake.

I couldn't sleep for weeks — I would have nightmares about Louis' body covered with blood . . . I didn't think about Louis in '76, but now I've been seeing him again. And I wonder what he would be doing now if that shell had landed on me and not on him? Would he have a family? Would he have a son?

When I see Louis now, I'm not afraid. I look at the blood and that's what I think about. Every minute of life blood is pumping through us, but for the first time now, as my life is ending, I am thinking about the blood that keeps me alive . . . and is killing me.

Blood.

Blood hound. Blood money. Blood lust. Blood pressure. Red blood. Blue blood. Blood feud. Blood sausage. Pool of blood. Blood bath. Blood cell. Sell blood. Blood steam. Draw blood. Blood thirsty. Blood sucking. Bloody fool! Blood libel. Blood bank. Pay in blood. Signed in blood. Blood curdling. Blood pudding. Bleeding heart liberals! Bloody Mary . . . the blood of Christ. *(Harder)* Mixed blood. Bad blood. Red blood. Blood red sunset of my life . . . Blood brothers, blood relatives . . . life blood.

Death blood.

DIALOGS

for One Man and One Woman

ALBUM

by
DAVID RIMMER

Album follows the relationships between four high school kids in the mid-1960s. The present scene titled "Runaway," takes place at 2:00 a.m. in a room in the Paradise Motel. It is after a dance, the night before graduation in June, 1967. Boo has an obsession with Bob Dylan, and Trish loves to listen to the Beatles; both are eighteen. Earlier the same evening, hiding out in the teachers' lounge, Boo promised to let her hear his new album of "Sgt. Pepper's Lonely Hearts Club Band," and they decided to run away — at least temporarily. He stole the radio from the teachers' lounge, and they both went to their homes, planning to meet later at the motel. When the following sequence begins, Trish has just joined Boo in the room by climbing through the window.

Album was first presented at Cherry Lane Theatre in New York City on October 1, 1980.

The full text of the play was published by Nelson Doubleday, Garden City, New York, in 1980. It is also available in an acting edition from Dramatists Play Service, 440 Park Avenue South, New York, New York 10016.

Reprinted by permission of David Rimmer. Copyright © 1981.

BOO: *(Laughs, jumps exuberantly on the bed. Sunglasses on.)*
This is so cool! The Paradise Motel . . . First time I've ever been in a motel, first time I ever stole a car —
TRISH: Your parents' —
BOO: First time I ever ran away, first time —
TRISH: You have to keep saying that?
BOO: What? First time? *(Smiles)*
TRISH: Don't look. *(She goes behind the closet door, taking the suitcase. He waits nervously, trying to be cool. He pulls down the bedspread, finds something on the sheet, flicks it away, arranges things neatly. Then he takes his guitar out of the case, and begins strumming and singing in Bob Dylan style the chorus of "Just Like a Woman.")*

BOO: *(Still strumming, makes the line part of the song.)* ... Takin' that dress off, huh? ... *(She comes out, wearing a pair of jeans and a loose-fitting peasant-type blouse, and holding onto her mother's album. He puts the guitar down, takes off the sunglasses and turns to her in anticipation. Disappointed.)* Oh. God, what you got in there? You're holdin' it like it was Fort Knox.

TRISH: Nothin'.

BOO: You don't want me to see?

TRISH: If this place is so cool, how come they don't have a TV?

BOO: *(Hurt)* Whaddaya think we're gonna do, watch TV all night?

TRISH: And the bathroom's down the hall?

BOO: What'd you expect, all the comforts of home?

TRISH: *(At the radio)* I don't know why you had to steal this. I s'pose you think you're John Dillinger or sombody ...

BOO: *(Little smile)* John Dillinger? ... It's possible. *(He starts prowling around the room; finds the Bible; leafs through it.)*

TRISH: What're you looking for?

BOO: Drugs. I thought somebody left some drugs in it.

TRISH: In the Bible?!

BOO: Maybe a band stayed here. That's where they stay when they're on the road — motels. And that's where they hide their stuff — Bibles. They hollow 'em out — *(Heads for the closet.)*

TRISH: What would a band be doin' around here? Playing at the Army Base? You lookin' for drugs in the closet?

BOO: Found a dime.

TRISH: Great place for a band. I met a guy in a band once. He knew a guy who knew a guy who knew the Beatles.

BOO: *(Sunglasses on; Dylan voice)* Ooooo, I'm impressed —

TRISH: He told me the original title of "Yesterday" was "Scrambled Eggs." *(She sings a couple of lines of the Beatles' "Yesterday," substituing "Scrambled Eggs" for "Yesterday." He tries to kiss her; she ducks. She picks up the copy of "Sgt. Pepper.")* We can't even play the album. That was dumb, you know, goin' up and gettin' this. You coulda got caught so easy.

BOO: I had to get the car keys, didn't I? What's the difference?

TRISH: The car keys were downstairs and the album was upstairs.

BOO: And my parents were asleep. Big deal.

TRISH: *(Reading the back of the album)* I read the news today . . .

BOO: *(Sunglasses off)* You know what was cool? When we first came onto the highway, and seein' it stretch out like that, and then just takin' off . . .

TRISH: Yeah. The lights were nice.

BOO: . . . I kept seein' this vision of the car cracked up, right in the middle of the highway. It was beautiful, kinda. You know, Dylan had this motorcycle accident where he almost got killed.

TRISH: That means we should do it too?

BOO: And I kept takin' my hands off the wheel. Closin' my eyes and driftin' like there was some kind of spell on me.

TRISH: Do me a favor, don't let me fall asleep next time I get in a car with you.

BOO: I didn't do anything.

TRISH: Thanks!

BOO: You looked nice asleep.

TRISH: I wasn't just sleeping! You're not the only one who has *visions* and all that stuff!

BOO: No — I know — I —

TRISH: I kept seeing myself in this big wheat field in Kansas. And everything was in black and white. All the people, and the crows. And the scarecrow kept saying to me, "There's no place like home, there's no place like home." We're not goin' to Kansas, are we?

BOO: Nah . . .

TRISH: Good. We goin' to California?

BOO: I dunno. Maybe.

TRISH: Where *are* we goin'?

BOO: I dunno where we're goin'. We're just goin'! OK? Trust me.

TRISH: OK, maybe I'll just *go* to my graduation tomorrow.

BOO: What do you mean?

TRISH: I wanna go back.

BOO: We just got here!

TRISH: I don't care. I wanna go home.

BOO: I thought you hated it there.

TRISH: You think I want to live here? You think this is an improvement? *(He stalks around the room, pacing vehemently, ignoring her. She softens, tries to reach him.)* Hey, we don't have to run away.

BOO: Maybe *you* don't.

TRISH: You don't either. Look, our mothers and fathers are still gonna be our mothers and fathers if we run away or not!

BOO: *(Dylan. Sunglasses on.)* Not a chance!

TRISH: Will you stop it?! You're just hiding behind that!

BOO: *(Bitter)* Hidin' from you.

TRISH: *(Quieter; reasonable)* We can go back. Nobody'll know where we've been.

BOO: *(Anger bursting out)* I want *everybody* to know where we've been!

TRISH: *(Angry back)* Yeah, if we have a "tragic accident" they'll know, they'll read it in the papers! "Two runaway teenagers killed in fiery crash" — that's what *you* want?

BOO: That's what happened to James Dean and all those guys, and Dylan almost, I bet he wanted it to —

TRISH: That's the stupidest thing I've ever heard! You think I'm getting into a car with you again, you're crazy! I'd rather call my parents — I'd rather call the police —

BOO: *Police?* We're *criminals* now!

TRISH: You're not *criminals* 'cause you steal your parents' car!

BOO: Shut up! *(She goes and sits on the bed, as far away from him as possible. Tense pause. He paces in small, nervous circles. She watches him warily. He stops, looks at her, sits at the foot of the bed, trying to be gentle, taking his sunglasses off.)* Hey, I — *(She quickly takes the pillows from the bed and places them between him and her. Instantly enraged, he grabs them and flings them aside. She flinches and moves further away, cringing against the wall, reaching out and grabbing for her photo album.)* What's in there, your baby pictures? *(He grabs it, picks it up. She grabs for it, and they struggle. He pulls away with it and looks inside.)* Hey, I remember this!

TRISH: *(Furious; shocked; frightened)* What do you mean, you remember this?!

BOO: You had all the Beach Boys songs in it —

TRISH: You follow me home from school, you go through my drawers, you gonna put *Dragnet* on my trail next? You're worse than my mother!

BOO: *(Flipping through the pages)* These're all Beatles songs —

TRISH: Give it back!

BOO: What's this? You write this?

TRISH: Don't read that! I don't want anybody to read that! *(She rushes up to him, but he fends her off.)*

BOO: What is it, your love book? Your diary? What'd you write?

TRISH: None of your business!

BOO: *(He yanks it away from her, shoves her, holds it toward the window as if to throw it out.)* Either I read it or nobody does!

TRISH: *(Stumbling away; very emotional; feels beaten)* **Don't!
It's my mother's.**

BOO: **I thought you hated her.**

TRISH: *(Frustrated; confused)* **I — no, I — I wanna go
home!**

BOO: *(Angry; bitter)* **No place like home!**

TRISH: *(Almost crying)* **I wanna go! I wanna see my dog . . .**

BOO: *(Throws the photo album down.)* **We haven't done
anything yet!**

TRISH: **I'll die before I do anything with you!**

BOO: *(Dylan voice: vicious, spits it out; sunglasses on)* **You
told me — wanted to hold me. You just ain't that
strong —** *(TRISH screams in frustration; yells back at
him, her strength returning.)*

TRISH: **I read the news today —**

BOO: *(Wild, insane Dylan; overlapping)* **Anybody can be
like me —**

TRISH: **A lucky man — made the grade —**

BOO: **But nobody can be like you — luckily —**

TRISH: **Blew his mind — the lights changed —**

BOO: **How's it feel — you're on your own —**

TRISH: *(Hands over her ears. Screaming)* **Scrambled eggs
— Love's an easy game to play —**

BOO: **No home —** *a rolling stone!*

TRISH: *(Chokes back tears of rage.)* ***Stop it!*** *(She suddenly
runs to the door, fumbles with the handle, can't get it open,
starts banging on it wildly.)*

BOO: **Shut up! You'll wake the whole place up!**

TRISH: **I'll scream so loud I'll wake the whole world up!**
*(He catches her, they struggle, he throws her roughly onto
the bed. She scrambles up and stands at the head of the
bed, like a cornered animal. He moves toward her to get
her to shut up.)* ***Get away from me!*** **Don't come near
me!** ***Help!*** *(Just as she screams, he rushes over and turns
on the radio as loud as it can go. The loud instrumental
part of the Beatles' "Good Morning Good Morning" blasts*

*out.) **Help!** I know why you did that — you did that so nobody'll hear me when you —*

BOO: **What?**

TRISH: **I've seen it in the movies, don't deny it —**

BOO: **When I what?**

TRISH: **Don't deny it!**

BOO: **Deny what?!** *(He jumps onto the bed. They both stand there, hysterical, screaming at each other over the music.) (The following dialog is spoken simultaneously.)*

BOO: **When I what? Dare what? What'm I gonna do? *What?* When I what?**

TRISH: **Don't you dare! Shut up! You better not — I don't know! I don't know! *I don't know!*** *(He yanks the radio out of its socket and throws it down on the floor with a loud crash. She dissolves into tears.)*

BOO: **OK! OK!** *(Still frustrated, he punches the wall, hurting his hand. Stops, turns to her, almost crying.)* **What'd you think I was gonna do —?** *(He can't finish; breaks off with a sob; hides his face. She moves closer to him. He lifts his face slowly.)* **I don't need any music.** *(He kneels on the floor, beginning to break down. She kneels on the bed, getting nearer to him.)*

TRISH: **You don't have to be Bob Dylan. You don't have to be anybody.**

BOO: *(After a beat)* **We'll go home.**

TRISH: **Home? Never heard of it.** *(She pulls him to her and hugs him.)*

THE BREAKFAST SPE(

by
MATTHEW CALHOUN

This comic one-act play is printed he
setting is a seedy lower East Side diner ...
represented only by two beat-up folding chairs facing ..
about a table's distance apart. The Waitress is a not-too-mot-
vated functionary in her midtwenties. The Customer is a well-
turned-out gourmet in his late twenties.

Written during the author's playwrights residency at New
York's Thompkins Square Public Library, *The Breakfast Special*
was first produced off-off-Broadway in 1985 as part of a comic
revue called "Skits-ophrenia."

WAITRESS: Menu, sir?

CUSTOMER: No thanks. I know just what I want.

WAITRESS: Uh huh?

CUSTOMER: A robin egg omelette topped with coriander
made French style — *red* caviar in that, and a
licorice liqueur, please.

WAITRESS: Huh?

CUSTOMER: Yes, all that and some Wonder Bread toast
with wild gooseberry preserves. Shave the crusts,
please.

WAITRESS: We don't have that . . . here.

CUSTOMER: No Wonder Bread? You should try it. That
cheap, synthetic texture provides a delightful
contrast to some of the more docile of the wild
preserves. Wild raspberry needs more of a . . .

WAITRESS: We don't have those.

CUSTOMER: You mentioned that. Make it wild
blackberry then, and put it on Arnold brick oven

white. Broil it, though, please. It makes a subtler taste, broiled.

WAITRESS: We don't have that stuff. We have scrambled or fried, or we could poach it for you, and it comes with home fries and coffee. Or French toast, if you want.

CUSTOMER: What?

WAITRESS: This is a diner, not a French cookbook place. We don't have robin eggs. You can get a Denver omelette, if you want.

CUSTOMER: This is a diner, as you said. I'd like to dine. I don't understand your attitude.

WAITRESS: We don't have liqueurs. We got O. J. or grapefruit juice.

CUSTOMER: This is New York City, lady. Can't I get breakfast?

WAITRESS: Pancakes? Tomato juice? Cold cereal? We got that.

CUSTOMER: Where am I, in primitive colonial New England where all they know how to fix is turkey and succotash?

WAITRESS: It's summer. We don't have a Thanksgiving menu till November.

CUSTOMER: Don't you have *anything* here?

WAITRESS: *(Shrugging)* Yankee bean soup.

CUSTOMER: OK, OK, bring me a menu. I'll eat that.

WAITRESS: There are some nice more exotic restaurants in Midtown. You can get the D train right over . . .

CUSTOMER: I don't want to take a subway to get a little breakfast. I'm not on a safari here. I don't want to have to hunt lion to get a bite to eat.

WAITRESS: Lion?

CUSTOMER: I suppose next you'll be telling me I can't get a little fresh squeezed tangerine juice here.

WAITRESS: The restaurant two doors north'll give you fresh squeezed O. J. if you want.

CUSTOMER: I'm sure they could give me bubble gum freshly garnered from under their tables, too, but I don't *want* that.

WAITRESS: You are being entirely unreasonable. A small, unassuming, lower East Side diner and you come in here and expect Julia Child to cater to your every whim. You get eggs here. You get toast. You get home fries. You can have a donut if you want. Glazed or plain. That's what you get. If you don't like it, then go hire a cook and a butler and live in a mansion on a hill somewhere. OK?

CUSTOMER: *(Momentarily stunned)* You're right. I expect too much out of life. I always have. I'm a bit neurotic that way. I just want things right, that's all. But I have no right to force my outlandish expectations on others. *(Stands, hugs her.)* Thanks for the outburst. A fella has to be put in his place sometimes. *(Sits)* Bring me the breakfast special. Whatever it is. Thanks.

WAITRESS: You can't have the breakfast special because it's 11:02. You can only get it before 11. You should have ordered it when you sat down.

CUSTOMER: You're right. My fault. Two fried eggs, then. That'll be fine.

WAITRESS: White, whole wheat or rye?

CUSTOMER: You have whole wheat eggs?

WAITRESS: *(Irritated)* Toast.

CUSTOMER: Oh, I see. Anything's fine. Anything that's easiest.

WAITRESS: White?

CUSTOMER: Rye. *(Beat; worriedly)* If I'm not imposing.

WAITRESS: Rye. Coffee?

CUSTOMER: Sure.

WAITRESS: OK, then. *(She starts to exit.)*

CUSTOMER: Oh!

WAITRESS: What?

CUSTOMER: Could I maybe have a table here, to eat off of?

WAITRESS: A table, sir?

CUSTOMER: Well there's two chairs here, but no table. I hate to eat off my lap.

WAITRESS: Couldn't you just pull up the other chair?

CUSTOMER: Well ... *(Short pause.)*

WAITRESS: Maybe we should just come to your house and serve you breakfast in bed, huh?

CUSTOMER: *(Embarrassed)* **OK. Sorry.** *(He pulls up the chair.)* **Chair will be fine.**

WAITRESS: You can pick up breakfast in the kitchen in about twenty minutes.

CUSTOMER: Twenty minutes? For eggs?

WAITRESS: Whadaya think, sir, we're gonna have a foreman whip the cook to work at superhuman speed to kill himself on your eggs? You've *got* a chair, sir. You think *we* get to sit down?

CUSTOMER: But there's no customers here!

WAITRESS: Cook's a freelance writer. He writes comedy skits as he works. Slows him down a little. What are you, anti-art?

CUSTOMER: And what did you mean pick it up in the kitchen?

WAITRESS: In twenty minutes. Kitchen's over there, right past the communal bathroom.

CUSTOMER: Aren't you going to bring it to me?

WAITRESS: What am I, your slave? Would you show a little initiative around here?

CUSTOMER: *(Getting up)* **I'm leaving.**

WAITRESS: It's about time. Robin egg omelette.

CUSTOMER: Eat off chairs.

WAITRESS: Wild gooseberry jam.

CUSTOMER: Twenty minutes so the moron can write comedy skits.

(The follow dialog is spoken simultaneously.)

WAITRESS: *Red* caviar. Licorice liqueur. Shave the crusts. Cook it French style. Wants a table. Expects me to *wait* on him.

CUSTOMER: Pick it up myself in the kitchen past the communal bathroom. Don't even have Wonder Bread toast. Wants me to take a subway for breakfast. Don't even have tangerine juice! *(Lights fade to end scene.)*

THE DIVINERS

by

JIM LEONARD, JR.

The Diviners takes place in the mythical southern Indiana town of Zion during the early 1930s — the great depression. The play's central character, Buddy Layman, lives with his father (a mechanic) and his sixteen-year-old sister, Jenny Mae. Although Buddy, in his midteens, is retarded, he is also a widely reputed water witch who can find the best location for a well by using a divining rod. Into the lives of the Layman family comes a former preacher and current indigent from Kentucky — C. C. Showers. Ferris Layman hires Showers, and the man befriends Buddy and Jenny Mae. In the present scene from Act 2, Showers and Jenny Mae go fishing by the river.

The Diviners: A Play in Two Acts and Elegies was developed by the Hanover College Theatre Group, Hanover, Indiana. Its first professional production occurred at New York City's Circle Repertory Company in 1980.

The complete text of *The Diviners: A Play in Two Acts and Elegies* is available in an acting edition from Samuel French.

(SHOWERS and JENNIE MAE enter with cane poles, a worm can, etc. A solid green light washes across the stage; the river.)

JENNIE MAE: How long?

SHOWERS: This long at least.

JENNIE MAE: Oh, C. C.

SHOWERS: Well maybe this long. But I'll tell you that fish was a fighter. By the time we got him to shore and netted all right he liked to bruise up a good dozen men.

JENNIE MAE: Well, little sunfish and bluegills about all you can catch here. Fish bottom you might find a carp.

SHOWERS: Sure looks awful pretty.

JENNIE MAE: It's a nice spot for fishin'.

SHOWERS: Now look at this, will you? I just here touch bottom. Must get to ten or twelve foot just a couple yards out there.

JENNIE MAE: It gets awful deep towards the middle. Lota the boys like to come here and swim.

SHOWERS: Now if boys in Indiana are halfway like the boys in Kentucky, I wouldn't imagine they bother too much with swimsuits.

JENNIE MAE: Yeah, they're the same then.

SHOWERS: *(Smiles)* I had a feelin' they might be. When it comes to swimmin', I'm lucky to float. Do a little dog paddlin' — that's about it.

JENNIE MAE: I stick to wadin', myself.

SHOWERS: Be happy just dangling my toes in the water. Been a while, I tell you. Too long, I figure.

JENNIE MAE: I thought you fished all the time.

SHOWERS: Well, I used to when I was a kid anyway. But when I had a church I was so full a worry. I never found time to do nothin'.

JENNIE MAE: What'd you worry about?

SHOWERS: Everything.

JENNIE MAE: Oh . . .

SHOWERS: You name it, I worried over it. Like I'd see a family loadin' down and taking off for California — they'd say, "Pastor, we ain't got no room for the dog." Well, I'd worry a while, then I'd take the dog. Must had near to a dozen old hounds at once for a while. Good dogs, though. I'd line 'em all up in the front room and practice my preachin' on 'em. Dogs kinda like bein' talked at.

JENNIE MAE: Well you talk real nice.

SHOWERS: I talk too damn much, Jennie Mae.

JENNIE MAE: It's not your fault, C. C. It's the river. My mama used to say people sit by the water they can't help but be talkin'. River's kinda magic like that.

SHOWERS: Your mama was right.

JENNIE MAE: I don't think she ever liked any place so much as the river. Be down here every other day through the summer. And come fall — well you never been here in the fall, but when the leaves start to changin' and the air's gettin' cooler . . .

SHOWERS: Won't be too long now . . .

JENNIE MAE: And as long as you're here you might as well stay on through winter. Everything's nice in the spring.

SHOWERS: Sounds like I might have to stay.

JENNIE MAE: Less you're missin' Kentucky.

SHOWERS: Naw. I tell you what I do miss, though, is them dogs.

JENNIE MAE: What'd you do with 'em all?

SHOWERS: Well, right before I left I gave 'em all to my kids.

JENNIE MAE: You have kids in Kentucky?

SHOWERS: Oh yeah. Musta had a good couple dozen spread clear cross the country.

JENNIE MAE: Couple dozen?

SHOWERS: Don't get so darned riled, Jennie Mae. They were church kids.

JENNIE MAE: Well I ought to use you for bait, C. C. Showers, but I can't be so mean to the fish.

SHOWERS: You know what those bubbles are on the water there, don't you?

JENNIE MAE: Air, I imagine.

SHOWERS: Those bubbles right there?

JENNIE MAE: Yeah?

SHOWERS: All those millions and trillions of bubbles?

JENNIE MAE: What?

SHOWERS: Fish farts.

JENNIE MAE: Fish farts!

SHOWERS: Jennie Mae, there must be more fish in this

river than stars in the sky and we still ain't had a nibble worth a notice.

JENNIE MAE: Well, you'll never get a bite with no worm on your hook. Here. Let me put one on for you.

SHOWERS: Naw . . .

JENNIE MAE: I don't mind.

SHOWERS: No, then I'd end up havin' to take a fish off. And don't tell me you'd do that for me too.

JENNIE MAE: All right, I won't tell you.

SHOWERS: But you would, huh?

JENNIE MAE: If you want.

SHOWERS: *(Setting his pole down)* **Well . . . I'm happy just to sit by the water.**

JENNIE MAE: *(Setting her pole down)* **All right.** *(Pause)*

SHOWERS: You know, Jennie Mae . . . you know you're awful nice.

JENNIE MAE: Oh . . .

SHOWERS: Yeah, you are, and I been meanin' to tell you.

JENNIE MAE: You have?

SHOWERS: I sure have. You're real nice, Jennie Mae . . . and you're also . . . *(They are both about ready to kiss.)* . . . real young.

JENNIE MAE: I'm sixteen.

SHOWERS: I know. That's awful young, don't you think?

JENNIE MAE: I don't feel real young.

SHOWERS: Well you are. You don't know how young, Jennie Mae, let me tell you.

JENNIE MAE: My mother was only seventeen when she got married.

SHOWERS: Got married?

JENNIE MAE: Yeah.

SHOWERS: Listen, I think we better head back to the house now.

JENNIE MAE: But we just got here.

SHOWERS: I know, but it's gonna be dark before long

and I think we best get home before . . .

JENNIE MAE: Are you tired or somethin'?

SHOWERS: Miss Layman, I'm worn to a tee.

JENNIE MAE: You want your back rubbed?

SHOWERS: No. No, here now. Let me help you. *(He gives her his hand and helps her stand. They carry their shoes and poles off, etc.)*

JENNIE MAE: *(As he touches her)* Do you know much about Adam and Eve?

SHOWERS: Yeah . . . yeah, I've run into that story before.

JENNIE MAE: You have?

SHOWERS: Yeah, it's a good one all right. But I'm a little more partial to what comes right before. I kinda like all the light the whole story starts out with.

DOONESBURY

by
G. B. TRUDEAU

This staged version of *Doonesbury* is set in Walden Commune and other places familiar to readers of the comic strip. The following dialog and duet from Act 1, Scene 7, is self-explanatory.

Doonesbury: A Musical Comedy was first performed at the Biltmore Theater, New York City, on November 21, 1983.

The full text of the play has been published by Holt, Rinehart, and Winston, New York City, 1984. An original cast recording of the music is available from MCA Records.

From *Doonesbury: A Musical Comedy* by G. B. Trudeau. Reprinted by permission of G. B. Trudeau. Copyright © 1983, 1984.

MIKE: Boy, it's good to see you. You look great. *(MIKE helps J.J. off with her coat.)*

J.J.: You're lookin' pretty slick yourself, kid. Is she around?

MIKE: Joanie? Uh . . . no, she's out shopping.

J.J.: Look, I gotta be honest with you, Mike. I'm here because you're graduating. But if she gets on my case, I'm just splitting.

MIKE: Splitting? Hey, no, you don't want to do that. We got big plans today.

J.J.: We do?

MIKE: You better believe it. Here, take a look at this. *(MIKE picks up his schedule, snaps out a carbon copy, and hands it to her.)*

J.J.: What is it?

MIKE: Our weekend schedule. That's your copy. You can keep it.

J.J.: Oh. Thanks. Where's it start?

MIKE: Right here where it says "4:15, J.J. arrives at house." Of course, we'll have to adjust that now, won't we? Let me get you a pencil.

J.J.: *(Reading)* "4:15, J.J. arrives at house; 4:20-4:25, Mike gets dinner in the oven while J.J. unwinds with a fast glass of wine . . ."

MIKE: Well, it doesn't have to be wine. This thing's pretty flexible. Anyway, at 4:30 sharp, after you finish unwinding, we go over to the quad for the big senior class softball game, which should be over by 6:10. Then from 6:15 to 6:45, I finish up dinner while you get to know my friends a little better so they won't think of you as a mere appendage of me but actually accept you as a person in your own right. OK. Now, that's followed at 7:00 by —

J.J.: Michael, wait a minute. This is a little overwhelming. What if we feel like just doing nothing, you know, just sitting out on the porch, not saying a word?

MIKE: 11:15 to 11:45. I'm way ahead of you.

J.J.: Michael, have you planned out your whole life this way?

MIKE: My whole life? Don't be silly. *(A beat)* Some of it.

J.J.: Like what?

MIKE: Um . . . well, you know about business school, of course. As for the rest . . . well, you know . . . nothing definite. It depends.

J.J.: Yeah, same with me. It depends.

BOTH: *(Sing)* I've been thinking . . . what?

J.J.: *(Sings)* No, please, please, go ahead, you were saying . . .

MIKE: *(Sings)* I was talking off the top of my head. I just thought . . .

J.J.: *(Sings)* You just thought . . .

MIKE: *(Sings)* That I might move on.

J.J.: *(Sings)* Really.

MIKE: *(Sings)* Find some sort of place Of my own whereupon

I was thinking . . .

J.J.: *(Sings)* You were thinking . . .

MIKE: *(Sings)* Well, I guess that I was hoping . . .

J.J.: *(Sings)* Hoping what?

MIKE: *(Sings)* No. It's dumb.

We'll be too busy coping,

There's all sorts of problems for us to weather,

But sometime soon we should try

To get together,

If it's OK with you.

J.J.: "Get together"?

MIKE: *(Sings)* Spend a few days with you.

BOTH: *(Sing)* Yeah, sometime soon we should try to get together.

MIKE: So, how about you?

J.J.: Well . . . *(Sings)* I found a studio apartment

Over by the art school,

Haven't signed the lease yet . . .

MIKE: *(Sings)* Hey, that's cool,

I can understand that

You need to be a . . .

J.J.: *(Sings)* A person in my own right.

MIKE: *(Sings)* I completely agree.

You should have your own friends . . .

J.J.: *(Sings)* I'm bound to make a few . . .

MIKE: *(Sings)* We shouldn't be like bookends,

Don't you think that's true?

J.J.: *(Sings)* I should go it alone,

If that's OK with you.

But sometime soon we should try

To get together . . .

MIKE: *(Sings)* Like to see you some more . . .

J.J.: *(Sings)* Get together . . .

MIKE: *(Sings)* I could sleep on the floor.

BOTH: *(Sing)* Yeah, sometime soon we should try to get together.

Oh, I've known since I found you,
I want to be around you,
But not be in your way,
We'll take it day by day.
Oh, I'll always be there for you,
It turns out I adore you,
So if I'm passing by,
I might give you a try.

J.J.: *(Sings)* And sometime soon we should try to get together . . .

MIKE: *(Sings)* Sometime soon we should try to get together.

BOTH: *(Sing)* Oooo, try to get together.

HOW I GOT THAT STORY

by
AMLIN GRAY

This play takes place in a southeast Asian country called Am-Bo Land where the USA is helping the government in its war against guerrilla insurgents. The play has only two actors; one plays the Reporter, who is in his late twenties, and the other, a male, plays all the other roles, including Americans and Ambonese, men and women, young people and old. In the present scene, titled "Imprintment," the Reporter, who has been wounded in the rump, is visited in the hospital by a local bar girl, Li. Kingsley, to whom the Reporter speaks at the end of the scene, is his boss from the news agency.

How I Got That Story was first performed by the Milwaukee Repertory Theater on April 12, 1979.

The full text of the play is available in an acting edition from Dramatists Play Service, Inc.; it has also been published by Nelson Doubleday (Garden City, New York) and also in James Reston, Jr., ed. *Coming to Terms: American Plays & the Vietnam War.* New York: Theatre Communications Group, 1985.

(A knock comes at the door — a very soft one. The REPORTER doesn't register it, but he stirs, rearranges himself for more sleep — sees the audience.)

REPORTER: **Where am I?** *(He sits partway up and feels a rush of pain.)* **Ow! Excuse me.** *(Discreetly, he lifts the sheet and turns his hip; remembers.)* **Oh yeah. What day is this? The last thing I remember is the medic and the morphine. I should find out where I am.** *(He makes a move to get up; stops mid-motion.)* **I feel dizzy.** *(The soft* knock is repeated.) **Come in?** *(LI enters: a small, pretty Ambonese bar girl. She walks with little steps into the room.)* **Hello.**

LI: **You sleep?**

REPORTER: **No, I'm awake. Are you the nurse?**

LI: **My name Li. Bar girl. I work Coral Bar. You know?**

REPORTER: **Um — no, I've never been there.**

LI: **I come here too. Man downstairs who sometime let me in. Are you G.I.?**

REPORTER: **No.**

LI: **See? I know you not G.I. I like you better than G.I.** *(Coming further into the room)* **You very nice.**

REPORTER: *(Holding her off)* **No, I'm not nice. I'm a reporter.**

LI: **Li not understand.**

REPORTER: **I'm someone who's not here — who's here but can't — do anything, except report.**

LI: *(Puzzled)* **You like I go away?**

REPORTER: **No, you don't have to go away . . .**

LI: **You lonely.**

REPORTER: **No I'm not. Not** *lonely* **. . .**

LI: **Yes, you lonely. I see.**

REPORTER: **I'm** *alone.* **It's a condition of the job.**

LI: **You tired.**

REPORTER: **Well, they've given me some medication . . .**

LI: **You lie down.**

REPORTER: **I'm lying down.**

LI: **You lie down all the way —**

REPORTER: *(Escapes by jumping out of bed — he is wearing blue institutional pajamas.)* **I've got a wonderful idea.**

LI: **No, where you go?**

REPORTER: **You sit down. Sit down on the bed.** *(Going into the pockets of his field clothes)* **Look, here's some money for your time. There's fifty** *hoi.* **Is that enough? I'm going to interview you.**

LI: *(Not knowing the word)* **In-ter-view?** *(The REPORTER* *has laid two small colored bills on the bed. LI picks them up and, somewhat uncertainly, sits down on the bed. The REPORTER sets up his tape recorder.)*

REPORTER: I've been feeling lately quite confused. I think that maybe, if I just can try and understand one person who's involved in all this, then I might be onto something. Will you tell me your story?

LI: Oh, you like me tell you story. Now I see. I have G.I. friend teach me tell him your Jack and the Beanstalk. When I get to part where beanstalk grow I stop and he say "Fee Fi Fo Fum" —

REPORTER: Not that kind of story. Just your life. Where do you come from?

LI: Where you like I come from?

REPORTER: From wherever you were born.

LI: OK. I try. *(Thinks a second, sizing the REPORTER up.)* I was born in little village. I hate the guerrillas. Was so glad when many helicopters come all full of big Americans. Americans with big guns. You have gun?

REPORTER: No.

LI: Yes, you do. I know you have gun.

REPORTER: No, I don't.

LI: Yes, great big huge big gun and shoot so straight —

REPORTER: *(Turns off the tape.)* No, no. That isn't what I want, Li. I just want your story. Nothing else.

LI: You shy.

REPORTER: It's just a question of professional procedure.

LI: You like woman to be like a man. I see now. Now I tell my story.

REPORTER: Wait. *(He switches on his tape.)* Go.

LI: I am spy. My name not Li at all.

REPORTER: What is it?

LI: My name *Gad Da Lai I Rang Toi Doung*. That mean Woman Who Love to Watch Foreigners Die. I hate Americans.

REPORTER: Now we're getting down to cases. I'll bet all you girls hate Americans.

LI: *(Encouraged)* Yes. I love to kill them.

REPORTER: Have you killed very many?

LI: Every day I kill one or I no can sleep. I like to pull their veins out with my little white sharp teeth. This is only thing can make Li happy with a man.

REPORTER: *(Getting drawn in)* Wow. That's *political*.

LI: I like to climb on top of you and bite you, chew your neck until your bones are in my teeth and then I crack them —

REPORTER: Stop! You're making this up too. Li, don't you understand? I want your real story. *(LI has found the light switch on the wall above the bed and turned it off.)* Li, turn the lights back on.

LI: You tired.

REPORTER: I'm not tired, I just *feel* tired.

LI: You come here.

REPORTER: I'll bring the tape recorder and we'll talk some more.

LI: You like it in my country?

REPORTER: *(Sitting on the bed)* No. I hate it. I don't understand what anybody's doing. I don't like it here at all.

LI: You like I turn lights on?

REPORTER: Yes.

LI: There. *(The lights are still off.)*

REPORTER: There what?

LI: You no see lights? Then you have eyes closed.

REPORTER: No —

LI: I turn lights off again. *(She leaves them off.)* You like that?

REPORTER: Are they on or off?

LI: You lie down.

REPORTER: *(Does)* Do you wear sunglasses indoors? At Mimi's all the girls wear very dark dark glasses. Are you touching me? You're not supposed to touch me.

LI: I no touch you. *(She is touching him.)*

REPORTER: I saw a man burn with a lot of people watching. I saw Ing dance. I was in the jungle and a piece of flying metal flew so fast you couldn't see it but it stopped inside my body. I'm in Am-Bo Land. *(The phone rings.)* The phone? *(He picks it up.)* Hello? *(Pause)* Mr. Kingsley, yes, hello! *(Pause)* You're here? Wait just a little second, Mr. Kingsley. *(Turning the lights on.)* Li? *(She is gone. The REPORTER looks puzzled but relieved. He takes the phone back up — interrupts his movement to make a quick check under the bed, but LI is truly gone. Into the phone.)* I'm sorry, sir — Hello?

THE MOUND BUILDERS

by
LANFORD WILSON

The central action of *The Mound Builders* takes place at an archeological site in southern Illinois during a summer dig. The crew, led by August Howe and his assistant, Dr. Dan Loggins, is excavating a series of large mounds built up by prehistoric people. They are working fast because the site, owned by the father of twenty-five-year-old Chad Jasker, is gradually being covered by an artificial lake, part of a major land development. Dan has brought along his new and pregnant wife, Dr. Jean Loggins, a twenty-five-year-old gynecologist. Jean was on the site the previous summer and met Chad at that time. In the present scene from Act 1, Chad takes the first opportunity he has to try to initiate a relationship with Jean.

The Mound Builders was first presented by the Circle Repertory Company in New York City on February 2, 1975.

The full text of *The Mound Builders* has been published by Hill and Wang, New York City.

Reprinted by permission of Hill and Wang, a division of Farrar, Straus and Giroux, Inc.: Excerpt from *The Mound Builders* by Lanford Wilson. Copyright © 1976 by Lanford Wilson.

CHAD: Last summer I didn't really figure you to marry Dan. You seemed to be pretty sure of what you wanted.

JEAN: Dan and I wanted more or less the same thing, I think.

CHAD: I tell you what, I got the car out front; there's something I want to show you.

JEAN: I don't think so.

CHAD: You don't even know what it is.

JEAN: I know, but nevertheless —

CHAD: You only live once.

JEAN: I'm not sure that's been proved.

CHAD: The courthouse. What can happen? Who's gonna miss you?

JEAN: I've seen it.

CHAD: Inside?
JEAN: No, I haven't been inside.
CHAD: See, now, you don't know. I want to show you.
JEAN: What?
CHAD: Will you come?
JEAN: No. I can't, Chad; what?
CHAD: You'll promise to see it?
JEAN: When I go into town again.
CHAD: There's a model of damn near the whole county laid out — it's huge — guess what it's called? The whole model —
JEAN: I can't guess, I really don't think —
CHAD: *(Overlapping)* OK, OK, I'm not playing with you — you promised. It's called Jasker's Development. The Jasker Development. They got . . . the hills, they got all the buildings, the mounds are on it — the ones that are left — they even got little trees set up — and this big, beautiful blue lake — like — not round, but maple-shaped, hand-shaped. We been talking six years to get Washington to give it to us.
JEAN: The mounds that are left?
CHAD: Four of them will be left, the other five the Interstate will take out. It's all part and parcel with the development. The lake and the new Interstate. See, we got 57 from Chicago already, which they're widening, and the new Interstate cuts across us the other way with all these interchanges — and all. It all goes — aw, hell, it'll just take fifteen minutes to see the damn model and understand what's happening.
JEAN: No, I'm sure. You can feel it. We're an anachronism. Squint your eyes and you can already see girls water skiing over the tops of the hawthorn trees. Restaurants with dance bands. It's all changing. The lake has become the fact, hasn't it?
CHAD: Pretty much.

JEAN: And you'll own a lot of the shoreline, won't you?

CHAD: Good piece. I could show you if we —

JEAN: Come on, really —

CHAD: Well, it's not how much we own, it's where it is. See — Dad was smart enough not to sell. Only thing he ever did — Guys were coming down from Memphis — See, we're sitting on the lake and the interchange.

JEAN: So you're right in the middle of it.

CHAD: We *are* the middle of it — we didn't even know. You wouldn't recognize this town if you'd seen it five years ago. Like, it didn't start being a tourist attraction till a few years ago; but all of a sudden Lily-Tulip is buying up twenty acres to build a new home office, a national headquarters with landscaping, and another one — a box company — cardboard boxes, and everybody's trying to buy our place. These guys from Memphis are talking to brokers and the brokers are driving out to chew it over with us, you know. And their offer goes up and it goes up, Dad just sits tight on it — and finally these guys come down to talk to us themselves, and they say, all right, you're not going to sell — you got the place we want to build on. What would you say about giving us a lease?

JEAN: Oh . . . that could mean a lot more.

CHAD: Every month, month on month for as long as they're in operation. They've been working over a year. Memphis is the main office of the Holiday Inn people. They've got their market studies, their books full of figures, they've got their artists' concept drawings already. They've got their eight hundred unit motel, they've got their swimming pools, and the facilities to the lake, they've got a layout would amaze . . . *(Floating)* Dream of something. Dream of something you want . . . anything. A restaurant with twenty-four-hour service — dream of anything you want. They showed us rug samples that thick — with padding under it. See, we're sitting on the lake and the interchange.

JEAN: All first-class stuff.

CHAD: A barber sh — ah, beauty parlor. A uh — the clubs, the little — with clubs . . .

JEAN: Sauna?

CHAD: No, you hit the damn ball, the little setup for a —

JEAN: Tennis court?

CHAD: Tennis court, too, but those — oh, shit. Golf! Little golf —

JEAN: Miniature golf.

CHAD: No, that's kids, that's toys — Chip and putt! Chip and putt. For practicing.

JEAN: Never heard of it.

CHAD: It's like where you learn, you practice — you never heard of it! I never had a golf club in my hand! There's a golf course at Marion, eighty miles off, probably the closest place you could go — I probably couldn't hit — *(Enjoying himself, nearly laughing)* I'd dig up the green; they'd kick me off the — but I'm going to! Hell! Go out chipping and putting; get me a pair of the shorts and the socks and the cap and those gloves they wear — Chip and putt with the pros, man. Lee Trevinos.

JEAN: You'll be terrific.

CHAD: You know what we get? Three per cent. On every dollar spent.

JEAN: That's amazing; that's a lot.

CHAD: Of everything except food. One per cent on food and drink . . . that's the deal they're offering us.

JEAN: You will be rich. That's what I find so profound about politics; the grace notes of that kind of power. The signing of an energy bill in Washington transforms rural areas into resorts — field hands into busboys.

CHAD: Yeah.

JEAN: They shall beat their plowshares into Pontiacs.

CHAD: *(Almost holding his breath)* I . . . got six acres all my own. For a house. On an island. I got an island — it will be. Out a little bit on the lake. Looks right across to it. Be able to sit on the lawn and watch people drive up off there to the motel — say that's another ten bucks. That guy over there's havin' himself a beer, that's two cents!

JEAN: *(A long pause; as she starts to move.)* You'll get a kick out of it.

CHAD: Hey . . . *(She stops.)* I'll give it to you . . . Anything you want, it's yours. I'll sign it over. You're the only thing I ever saw I really wanted.

JEAN: *(Long pause)* No.

CHAD: I want you to —

JEAN: Chad — get lost.

SHE STOOPS TO CONQUER

by

OLIVER GOLDSMITH

In this comedy, Charles Marlow, a young Londoner, comes out to the country to meet Miss Kate Hardcastle, the daughter of an old friend of his father. His father has arranged this meeting hoping to involve him in a permanent relationship and cure him of his loose ways with women. Although Charles is lively and witty with easy women, he finds it impossible to relate to honorable ladies of his own class. Tony Lumpkin, Kate's step-brother, meets Charles in a tavern and directs him to the Hardcastle estate; for a joke, however, he tells Marlow that the house is an inn. Charles, therefore, treats Kate's father like an innkeeper, much to the old man's outrage. In the one meeting Charles has with Kate, his inability to look directly at a woman of good breeding, combined with her large, face-concealing bonnet, keeps him from seeing her well enough to recognize her again. In the present scene from Act 3, Kate has learned about Tony's gag and has decided to meet Charles in the guise of a serving girl; in this way, by taking on the identity of a servant, she stoops to conquer. In Kate's first speech the Lion, the Angel, and the Lamb are names of guest rooms in the supposed inn.

She Stoops to Conquer was first performed at London's Covent Garden Theatre in 1773.

The full text of *She Stoops to Conquer* has been printed frequently and is available in single copies and anthologies of drama.

MISS HARDCASTLE: **Never fear me. I think I have got the true bar cant. — Did your honor call? — Attend the Lion there. — Pipes and tobacco for the Angel. — The Lamb has been outrageous this half hour . . .**
(Enter MARLOW.)

MARLOW: **What a bawling in every part of the house; I have scarce a moment's repose. If I go to the best room, there I find my host and his story; if I fly to the gallery, there we have my hostess with her curtesy down to the ground. I have at last got a moment to myself, and now for recollection.** *(Walks and muses.)*

MISS HARDCASTLE: Did you call, sir? Did your honor call?

MARLOW: *(Musing)* As for Miss Hardcastle, she's too grave and sentimental for me.

MISS HARDCASTLE: Did your honor call? *(She still places herself before him, he turning away.)*

MARLOW: No, child! *(Musing)* Besides, from the glimpse I had of her, I think she squints.

MISS HARDCASTLE: I'm sure, sir, I heard the bell ring.

MARLOW: No, no! *(Musing)* I have pleased my father, however, by coming down, and I'll tomorrow please myself by returning. *(Taking out his tablets and perusing.)*

MISS HARDCASTLE: Perhaps the other gentleman called, sir?

MARLOW: I tell you no.

MISS HARDCASTLE: I should be glad to know, sir. We have such a parcel of servants.

MARLOW: No, no, I tell you. *(Looks full in her face.)* Yes, child, I think I did call. I wanted — I wanted — I vow, child, you are vastly handsome!

MISS HARDCASTLE: O la, sir, you'll make one ashamed.

MARLOW: Never saw a more sprightly, malicious eye. Yes, yes, my dear, I did call. Have you got any of your — a — what d'ye call it in the house?

MISS HARDCASTLE: No, sir, we have been out of that these ten days.

MARLOW: One may call in this house, I find, to very little purpose. Suppose I should call for a taste, just by way of trial, of the nectar of your lips; perhaps I might be disappointed in that too?

MISS HARDCASTLE: Nectar? Nectar? That's a liquor there's no call for in these parts. French, I suppose. We keep no French wines here, sir.

MARLOW: Of true English growth, I assure you.

MISS HARDCASTLE: Then it's odd I should not know it.

We brew all sorts of wines in this house, and I have lived here these eighteen years.

MARLOW: Eighteen years! Why, one would think, child, you kept the bar before you were born. How old are you?

MISS HARDCASTLE: O! sir, I must not tell my age. They say women and music should never be dated.

MARLOW: To guess at this distance, you can't be much above forty. *(Approaching)* Yet nearer, I don't think so much. *(Approaching)* By coming close to some women, they look younger still; but when we come very close indeed — *(Attempting to kiss her)*

MISS HARDCASTLE: Pray, sir, keep your distance. One would think you wanted to know one's age as they do horses, by mark of mouth.

MARLOW: I protest, child, you use me extremely ill. If you keep me at this distance, how is it possible you and I can be ever acquainted?

MISS HARDCASTLE: And who wants to be acquainted with you? I want no such acquaintance, not I. I'm sure you did not treat Miss Hardcastle, that was here a while ago, in this obstropalous manner. I'll warrant me, before her you looked dashed, and kept bowing to the ground, and talked, for all the world, as if you were before a justice of peace.

MARLOW: *(Aside)* Egad, she has hit it, sure enough! *(To her)* In awe of her, child? Ha! Ha! Ha! A mere awkward squinting thing! No, no! I find you don't know me. I laughed and rallied her a little; but I was unwilling to be too severe. No, I could not be too severe, curse me!

MISS HARDCASTLE: Oh, then, sir, you are a favorite, I find, among the ladies!

MARLOW: Yes, my dear, a great favorite. And yet, hang me, I don't see what they find in me to follow. At the Ladies' Club in town I'm called their agreeable Rattle.

Rattle, child, is not my real name, but one I'm known by. My name is Solomons; Mr. Solomons, my dear, at your service. *(Offering to salute her)*

MISS HARDCASTLE: Hold, sir; you are introducing me to your club, not to yourself. And you're so great a favorite there, you say?

MARLOW: Yes, my dear. There's Mrs. Mantrap, Lady Betty Blackleg, the Countess of Sligo, Mrs. Longhorns, old Miss Biddy Buckskin, and your humble servant, keep up the spirit of the place.

MISS HARDCASTLE: Then it's a very merry place, I suppose?

MARLOW: Yes, as merry as cards, suppers, wine, and old women can make us.

MISS HARDCASTLE: And their agreeable Rattle. Ha! Ha! Ha!

MARLOW: *(Aside)* Egad! I don't quite like this chit. She looks knowing, methinks. You laugh, child?

MISS HARDCASTLE: I can't but laugh to think what time they all have for minding their work or their family.

MARLOW: *(Aside)* All's well; she don't laugh at me. *(To her)* Do you ever work, child?

MISS HARDCASTLE: Ay, sure. There's not a screen or a quilt in the whole house but what can bear witness to that.

MARLOW: Odso! Then you must show me your embroidery. I embroider and draw patterns myself a little. If you want a judge of your work, you must apply to me. *(Seizing her hand)*

MISS HARDCASTLE: Ay, but the colors don't look well by candlelight. You shall see all in the morning.

SPOKESONG

by
STEWART PARKER

The play takes place in Belfast, Northern Ireland, during the early 1970s with flashbacks to the previous eighty years. The set represents Frank Stock's living room and bicycle shop and a street. Frank is a staunch advocate of the bicycle and a bitter opponent of the automobile. Just prior to the present scene at the beginning of Act 1, Frank has testified at a hearing into an urban redevelopment proposal; he spoke in favor of outlawing the automobile and rediscovering the bicycle. Now, alone at home, he continues to rhapsodize about the bicycle as Daisy enters his shop and his life.

Spokesong, or The Common Wheel was first presented in Ireland at the John Player Theatre at the Dublin Theatre Festival '75. Its American premiere occurred at the Long Wharf Theatre, New Haven, Connecticut, on February 2, 1978. The music "Daisy Bell" is the tune for the old song that goes "Daisy, Daisy, Give me your answer, do. I'm half crazy, All for the love of you. It won't be a stylish marriage — I can't afford a carriage. But you'll look sweet On the seat Of a bicycle built for two."

The full text of this play, *Spokesong, or The Common Wheel,* is available in an acting edition from Samuel French, Inc.

This scene from *Spokesong, or The Common Wheel* is reprinted by permission of the playwright's agent, London Management & Representation, Ltd. Book Copyright © 1979, 1980 by Stewart Parker.

FRANK: **Because it's been around so long, we overlook the miracle of it. Fastest form of urban transportation. Carries you a thousand miles on the food-energy equivalent of a gallon of petrol. Sixteen of them can fit into the space required to park one car.** *(DAISY comes through the door into the shop, pushing a ten-year-old rusty looking lady's bicycle.)* **And so on and so forth. They've no common sense, but statistics always impress them.** *(He goes up to behind the counter.)* **Hello and welcome.**

DAISY: **Do you repair bikes here?**

FRANK: At every opportunity, kid.

DAISY: This specimen here has been lying out in our back yard for years now.

FRANK: It's time you recycled it.

DAISY: It's rotten with rust.

FRANK: I'll take a look over it for you, if you like.

DAISY: I'm afraid it needs a lot more than looking over.

FRANK: A look, a smile, a lingering caress. It's crying out for a bit of loving attention, like the rest of us.

DAISY: So long as I can afford it.

FRANK: It'll be the best of value ...

DAISY: *(Walking to door)* When should I call back, then?

FRANK: ... especially for a teacher.

DAISY: *(Stopping)* You don't say.

FRANK: Not only well within your budget — but getting you to your work in a manner which compensates for its sedentary nature.

DAISY: There's nothing sedentary about the school I work in.

FRANK: In brief — a transport of delight.

DAISY: How did you guess my job?

FRANK: A certain chalk dust between index finger and thumb.

DAISY: So I've started looking like a teacher.

FRANK: A certain authority of manner.

DAISY: Elementary, no doubt.

FRANK: But yes ... Holmes was shaking his head. A bicycle, certainly, but not *the* bicycle, said he. I am familiar with forty-two different impressions left by tires. This, as you perceive, is a Dunlop, with a patch upon the outer cover. Heidigger's were Palmer's, leaving longitudinal stripes ... It is of course possible that a cunning man might change the tires of his bicycle in order to leave unfamiliar tracks. A criminal who is capable of such a thought is a man whom I should be proud to do business with.

DAISY: Thanks, we'll let you know.

FRANK: This bike's a good model.

DAISY: My grandparents bought me it. As a prize for conning my way into university.

FRANK: You couldn't have had it that many years, then.

DAISY: Ten. So that must make me about twenty-eight. OK? *(She goes through the door. He follows her as far as the door.)*

FRANK: Call in tomorrow same time. I can tell you then what needs doing.

DAISY: If there's a lot of work involved I might just buy a new one. I need it pretty quickly, my car died on me yesterday.

FRANK: One of a dying species — headed for extinction.

DAISY: Is that so? I suppose the bicycle is immortal.

FRANK: Bicycles are human, kid.

DAISY: *(Studies him.)* I'll leave you with my friend, then. *(Exits)*

FRANK: Till tomorrow. *(The piano bursts into "Daisy Bell." FRANK vaults back into the shop, picks up the bicycle by the frame, and waltzes around with it, then staggers and collapses to the floor with it on top of him. DAISY re-enters the shop. Silence.)*

DAISY: I never left you a name and address.

FRANK: Good thinking.

DAISY: I'll write it down here. *(She goes to the counter, produces pen and paper, and writes.)* Just in case I forget to call back. *(She finishes, walks back to the door, turns and looks at him.)* I take it this is the outcome of the look, the smile and the lingering caress. *(Exits. FRANK goes to the counter and picks up the piece of paper.)*

FRANK: *(Reading)* Margaret Bell ... Great Scott ... Oh, rapture ... Oh bliss ... an actual Daisy Bell! *(Music. He sweeps up the bicycle and sings to it, as he carries it down to the work area, puts it up on its stand, and removes the saddle.)* There is a flower within my heart, Daisy, Daisy,

Planted one day by a glancing dart
Planted by Daisy Bell.
Whether she loves me or loves me not
Sometimes it's hard to tell
Yet I am longing to share the lot
Of Beautiful Daisy Bell . . .
(He holds the saddle up and apostrophises it.)
 Would that I had been where thou hast been, kid.
(He replaces the saddle, sets the bicycle upside-down, and seats himself beside it. Lights dim on the shop area, and intensify on the work space.) **With trembling fingers he removed the spring clip from her chain —** *(Does so with pliers)* **and unhooked the connecting link —** *(Does so and removes chain)* **he gazed at last upon the ravishing yet strangely vulnerable symmetry of her crank assembly. A sense of wonder mingled with the swelling drumbeat of his desire, his hands sweeping across the firm young spokes, up, up to their nippleheads, until the soft pliant tires yielded to his touch and sent his senses spinning.**

'TIS PITY SHE'S A WHORE

by
JOHN FORD

Giovanni and Annabella, son and daughter of a citizen of Parma, Italy, named Florio, have been lovers for almost a year, and she is pregnant with his child. She has been forced into a marriage with the corrupt nobleman, Soranzo. Soranzo, who has discovered the incestuous relationship between the two, has invited Giovanni to the wedding feast and then arranged for him to be alone with Annabella. He plans to catch them making love and then have them murdered by assassins he has hired. After Giovanni kills Annabella in the scene printed here, he enters the dining room with her heart on his dagger and kills Soranzo before the assassins end his own life. The following dialog is the complete fifth scene of the play's fifth act.

'Tis Pity She's a Whore, first published in 1633, was performed by the Queens Servants acting company at Drury Lane Theatre in London.

The complete play was published by the University of Nebraska Press in 1966, by Hill and Wang in 1968, and by Methuen in 1975. It is also available in Havelock Ellis, ed. *John Ford: Five Plays.* New York: Hill and Wang, 1957.

GIOVANNI: What, changed so soon! Hath your new
    sprightly lord
  Found out a trick in night-games more than we
  Could know in our simplicity? Ha! Is't so?
  Or does the fit come on you, to prove treacherous
  To your past vows and oaths?
ANNABELLA: Why should you jest
  At my calamity, without all sense
  Of the approaching dangers you are in?
GIOVANNI: What danger's half so great as thy revolt?
  Thou art a faithless sister, else thou know'st,
  Malice, or any treachery beside,
  Would stoop to my bent brows: why, I hold fate
  Clasped in my fist, and could command the course
  Of time's eternal motion, hadst thou been

One thought more steady than an ebbing sea.
And what? You'll now be honest, that's resolved?
ANNABELLA: Brother, dear brother, know what I have
been,
And know that now there's but a dining-time
'Twixt us and our confusion: let's not waste
These precious hours in vain and useless speech.
Alas, these gay attires were not put on
But to some end; this sudden solemn feast
Was not ordained to riot in expense;
I, that have now been chambered here alone,
Barred of my guardian or of any else,
Am not for nothing at an instant freed
To fresh access. Be not deceived, my brother;
This banquet is an harbinger of death
To you and me; resolve yourself it is,
And be prepared to welcome it.
GIOVANNI: Well, then;
The schoolmen teach that all this globe of earth
Shall be consumed to ashes in a minute.
ANNABELLA: So I have read too.
GIOVANNI: But 'twere somewhat strange
To see the waters burn: could I believe
This might be true, I could believe as well
There might be hell or Heaven.
ANNABELLA: That's most certain.
GIOVANNI: A dream, a dream! Else in this other world
We should know one another.
ANNABELLA: So we shall.
GIOVANNI: Have you heard so?
ANNABELLA: For certain.
GIOVANNI: But d'ye think
That I shall see you there? — You look on me. —
May we kiss one another, prate or laugh,
Or do as we do here?
ANNABELLA: I know not that.

But, brother, for the present, what d'ye mean
To free yourself from danger? Some way think
How to escape: I'm sure the guests are come.
GIOVANNI: Look up, look here; what see you in my face?
ANNABELLA: Distraction and a troubled conscience.
GIOVANNI: Death, and a swift repining wrath: — yet
    look;
What see you in mine eyes?
ANNABELLA: Methinks you weep.
GIOVANNI: I do indeed: these are the funeral tears
    Shed on your grave; these furrowed-up my cheeks
    When first I loved and knew not how to woo.
    Fair Annabella, should I here repeat
    The story of my life, we might lose time.
    Be record all the spirits of the air,
    And all things else that are, that day and night,
    Early and late, the tribute which my heart
    Hath paid to Annabella's sacred love
    Hath been these tears, which are her mourners now!
    Never till now did Nature do her best
    To show a matchless beauty to the world,
    Which in an instant, ere it scarce was seen,
    The jealous Destinies required again.
    Pray, Annabella, pray! Since we must part,
    Go thou, white in thy soul, to fill a throne
    Of innocence and sanctity in Heaven.
    Pray, pray, my sister!
ANNABELLA: Then I see your drift. —
Ye blessed angels, guard me!
GIOVANNI: So say I.
    Kiss me. If ever after-times should hear
    Of our fast-knit affections, though perhaps
    The laws of conscience and of civil use
    May justly blame us, yet when they but know
    Our loves, that love will wipe away that rigor
    Which would in other incests be abhorred.

Give me your hand: how sweetly life doth run
In these well-colored veins! How constantly
These palms do promise health! But I could chide
With Nature for this cunning flattery.
Kiss me again: — forgive me.

ANNABELLA: With my heart.

GIOVANNI: Farewell!

ANNABELLA: Will you be gone?

GIOVANNI: Be dark, bright sun,
And make this midday night, that thy gilt rays
May not behold a deed will turn their splendor
More sooty than the poets feign their Styx!—
One other kiss, my sister.

ANNABELLA: What means this?

GIOVANNI: To save thy fame, and kill thee in a kiss.
(Stabs her.)
Thus die, and die by me, and by my hand!
Revenge is mine; honor doth love command.

ANNABELLA: O, brother, by your hand!

GIOVANNI: When thou art dead
I'll give my reasons for't; for to dispute
With thy — even in thy death — most lovely beauty,
Would make me stagger to perform this act,
Which I most glory in.

ANNABELLA: Forgive him, Heaven — and me my sins!
Farewell,
Brother unkind, unkind — Mercy, great Heaven!
O, O! *(Dies))*

GIOVANNI: She's dead, alas, good soul! The hapless fruit
That in her womb received its life from me
Hath had from me a cradle and a grave.
I must not dally. This sad marriage-bed,
In all her best, bore her alive and dead.
Soranzo, thou hast missed thy aim in this:
I have prevented now thy reaching plots,
And killed a love, for whose each drop of blood

I would have pawned my heart. — Fair Annabella,
How over-glorious art thou in thy wounds,
Triumphing over infamy and hate! —
Shrink not, courageous hand, stand up, my heart,
And boldly act my last and greater part!

ZEBRA

by
DALE DOERMAN

This one-act play is printed here in its entirety. The action
of the play takes place in a city park on a summer evening.
Kevin, in his midtwenties, is sitting near Helen, a peculiarly
attractive woman in her early thirties. Total strangers, they
are listening to a jazz jam. Kevin is talking to Helen, desperately
trying to be heard over the loud music. Helen is following the
gist of the conversation without working at it. The music ends,
and we hear them speak.

Zebra was first produced by Broadripple Theatre at the
Michigan Theatre Festival, Lakeside, Michigan, in 1984.

KEVIN: You don't hear that one very much. I haven't
anyway. Definitely classical.

HELEN: No, my friend. That is jazz.

KEVIN: Not the music. I meant your name. *(Pause)*
Helen.

HELEN: Yes ... classical ... I noticed that. *(Pause)* Well
... its certainly been nice ...

KEVIN: I was ...

HELEN: Yes?

KEVIN: ... was hoping that I could see you again.

HELEN: You were?

KEVIN: Kevin. My name is Kevin.

HELEN: I know. You said that. I really couldn't say yet
if that's possible. I couldn't go out with just anyone.
Not these days.

KEVIN: I understand.

HELEN: That's good! You have to be understanding.

KEVIN: Exactly.

HELEN: I must have understanding.

KEVIN: Me too. *(Pause)* I'm free tonight.

HELEN: I work tomorrow. *(Pause)*

KEVIN: I try to get out to the park every Sunday . . . I like watching people.

HELEN: . . . and the animals. I usually come in by the zoo.

KEVIN: Yeah?

HELEN: You can tell that some of them don't like being locked up in those cages.

KEVIN: Who would? It's inhumane.

HELEN: A good-sized zoo is a kind of United Nations for the wild kingdoms. If you think about it, that's what it is. That's how they see it. Each specimen is selected to represent their species. They do have the company of the other animals.

KEVIN: And people. They see lots of people every day. They stand there and make faces. They talk to them and feed them peanuts . . .

HELEN: I sang to the zebra once.

KEVIN: *(Laughing)* No kidding?

HELEN: It was fun. One of those crazy things that you do when other people aren't looking?

KEVIN: Did he like it?

HELEN: Who?

KEVIN: Zebra.

HELEN: I don't know for sure. It's difficult to say with a zebra.

KEVIN: Well, you tried anyway.

HELEN: I still do. I always stop and sing at least one verse of "On the Street Where You Live," whenever they have him out.

KEVIN: They say you can't get too much of a good thing.

HELEN: I can't tell if he's becoming more of an audience or a critic. Sometimes, when there's a crowd around, I'll gradually make my way to his cage. If I want, I'll stroll by the monkeys first. That brings me closer to the zebra and it doesn't look like I'm giving him preferential treatment.

KEVIN: Good idea.

HELEN: Last week I saw the zebra turn around and watch me at the monkey cage. I think that he was jealous.

KEVIN: He could be.

HELEN: Yes. I think so.

KEVIN: What did he do?

HELEN: From the corner of his eyes, he carefully observed my every move at the monkey cage. His head was cocked off in the direction of the crowd but his eyes were on me the whole time.

KEVIN: I've seen that.

HELEN: When I finished with the monkeys, I slowly turned away from his gaze and wandered to the far side of the cage behind him. He couldn't see me now unless he turned his body. The crowd was watching him. It was driving him crazy. Softly, I began to sing. "I have often walked on this street before, but the pavement's always stayed beneath my feet before."

There is this buzz of voices coming from the crowd. The zebra doesn't move.

"All at once am I . . ."

I hold the note.

". . . I — I — I — I — . . . several stories high, knowing I'm on the street where you live."

He can't stand it anymore. He begins this turn to the left side of his cage. The turn starts from his ears and he just keeps moving until he's totally into it and even his tail is running. He's beautiful! A masterpiece of motion! There is this flash of zebra moving behind the bars that separate our lives . . a maelstrom of lines and spaces and then he's there. Nose to nose with me at the edge of the cage. He sneezes in my face. The explosion sends this shock wave through his mane, to his torso, then his legs ... dissipating into the earth. *(Pause)*

I smile. I know that I have his undivided attention. *(Pause)*

KEVIN: What happens then?

HELEN: Nothing. It's already happened. *(Pause)*

KEVIN: You still see the zebra?

HELEN: When I need it. It's good for the soul. Sometimes I enjoy seeing the creatures caged up. It brings out the animal nature.

KEVIN: I can see how it would.

HELEN: In the wild, they're unpredictable. The cage makes them more human. *(Pause as KEVIN senses that his opportunity is somehow slipping away.)*

KEVIN: I have tickets for this jazz concert next weekend.

HELEN: I like jazz. All kinds. It does something to me. It does. Gets inside and lives there. Like a musical possession. *(Pause)* Why don't we get together for dinner one night? *(HELEN silences KEVIN's lips with her finger.)* Give me your number. *(KEVIN scrawls his phone number on a scrap of paper. HELEN watches him intently.)* I know this wonderful Romanian cafe that you've never been to. *(KEVIN hands HELEN the paper.)* Don't say anything. *(HELEN takes the phone number.)* I really have enjoyed communicating with you. *(HELEN exits gracefully leaving KEVIN spellbound.)*

DIALOGS

for Two Men

DEER DOGS

by
DAVID MAMET

This short play is presented here in its entirety. David Mamet's introductory stage direction says, "Two men, Larry and Bunchy, at a country store. There are also a couple of onlookers."

Deer Dogs is also available in David Mamet's *Goldberg Street: Short Plays & Monologues.* New York: Grove Press, 1985.

Deer Dogs is reprinted by permission of Grove Press, a division of Wheatland Corporation. Copyright © 1982 David Mamet.

LARRY: Dog's runnin' deer; it should be shot.

BUNCHY: But who's to tell it's runnin' deer? Law says you see a dog in pursuit of a deer you can shoot him. Who's to say it's ... wait, wait, you take Dave here: keeps his dog tied up. One day th' dog, say Larry Thompson's dog, is runnin' by — Dave's dog gets loose ... Larry's dog runnin' deer. Someone sees it and, down the road later on, Larry's dog and Dave's dog. What does he do? Shoot 'em both.

LARRY: How did Dave's dog get loose?

BUNCHY: ... I'm saying a dog which is usually tied down, Dave's dog ...

LARRY: How did it get loose?

BUNCHY: I'm saying one day when it is loose ... I don't know how it got loose ...

LARRY: And was it runnin' deer ...?

BUNCHY: No.

LARRY: How do you know?

BUNCHY: 'Cause it hasn't got a taste for them. It's a tame dog.

LARRY: How do you know?

BUNCHY: Well, now, now, now, because it is a tame dog: I, you know that dog ...

LARRY: ... I'm ...

BUNCHY: ... I know what you're ...

LARRY: I'm ...

BUNCHY: I know what you're, wait a second — I know what you're saying ... that the dog is, though the dog is tame, it gets loose it starts runnin' deer. Is that it?

LARRY: Yes.

BUNCHY: But what I'm saying, this case we know that the dog is tame. It's tame. It isn't runnin' deer. All right? It's Dave's dog. It's tame. It's been tied up constantly ...

LARRY: How does it ...

BUNCHY: ... that's not ...

LARRY: ... how does it get loose?

BUNCHY: Well, say that Dave forgot to tie it up.

LARRY: And where does it go?

BUNCHY: ... I ...

LARRY: Where does it go?

BUNCHY: I know what you're saying. It goes to the woods. All right.

LARRY: What is it doing there?

BUNCHY: It's out. With Larry Thompson's dog.

LARRY: What are they doing?

BUNCHY: Larry's dog is runnin' deer.

LARRY: And what is Dave's dog doing?

BUNCHY: I don't know.

LARRY: Well, I don't know either — but I'm going to assume it's runnin' deer. *(Pause)*

BUNCHY: Would you shoot it?

LARRY: Yes. I would.

BUNCHY: You'd shoot Dave's dog?

LARRY: Yes. I would. *(Pause)*

BUNCHY: *(Snorts)* You would shoot Dave's dog. *(Pause)*

LARRY: Yes. I would.

BUNCHY: Because you know that that's the dog that'll

be caught. Not Larry Thompson's dog. *(Pause)* **That's the dog that will be caught ... Shoot! It's a bad law ... I'm sorry.** *(Pause)* **I don't like it.**

LARRY: You'll like it when you go out in the woods there ain't no deer ...

BUNCHY: *(Pause)* **Nossir.** *(Pause)* **No** *sir* **... N' I'm going to tell you one more thing: What the law ... wait a second — what the law encourages a fella to do is — I'm not saying you or me, but what it sets a man up to do is to say, "I'm going to shoot that fella's dog." That's not right.** *(Pause)*

THE DIVINERS

by
JIM LEONARD, JR.

The Diviners takes place in the mythical southern Indiana town of Zion during the early 1930s — the great depression. The play's central character, Buddy Layman, lives with his father (a mechanic) and his sixteen-year-old sister, Jenny Mae. Buddy, in his midteens, is described in the play's cast list as an "idiot-boy." Buddy's central traits are innocence and vulnerability, a lack of coordination between his perceptions of the world, his intended responses, and the executing of his responses — an emotional and intellectual frustration. Buddy always speaks of himself in the third person. He has an uncanny and contradictory relationship with water; on the one hand, he is a water witch who can find the best location for a well by using a divining rod, and he can accurately prophesy the coming of rain; on the other hand, partly because his mother died by drowning in the river, he has an obsessive terror of water. Since he won't bathe, he has an itchy skin rash, especially on his feet and legs. Into the lives of the Layman family comes a former preacher and current indigent from Kentucky — C. C. Showers. Ferris Layman hires Showers, and the man befriends Buddy, teaches him about life, and doctors his rash. The current scene from the top of Act 2 shows the developing relationship between the two "diviners," Buddy and Showers.

The Diviners: A Play in Two Acts and Elegies was developed by the Hanover College Theatre Group, Hanover, Indiana. Its first professional production occurred at New York City's Circle Repertory Company in 1980.

The complete text of *The Diviners: A Play in Two Acts and Elegies* is available in an acting edition from Samuel French.

This excerpt from *The Diviners* is reprinted by permission of William Morris Agency, Inc., on behalf of the author. Copyright © 1980, 1981, 1983 Jim Leonard, Jr.

(Morning. Faint sounds of birds. As the light rises we see BUDDY creeping onto the stage, bent low with one hand held out as he tries to befriend a small bird.)

BUDDY: Ain't you so pretty, huh? Ain't you so pretty. You're the color a the sky. Yes, you are. You want a

be up there now, don't you? In the sun and the wind. Well, hold still now. Hold still. He ain't gonna hurt you. *(SHOWERS enters as the boy catches the bird.)* You're too little to fly. Shhh, you're all right.

SHOWERS: Is he hurt?

BUDDY: Look at him, C. C. He's little.

SHOWERS: It's an awful pretty bird.

BUDDY: See his feathers?

SHOWERS: Those're blue.

BUDDY: Blue?

SHOWERS: Blue like your eyes.

BUDDY: His eyes is blue?

SHOWERS: Like the bird, like the sky — that's all blue.

BUDDY: Boy. You want a lift him, C. C.? Put him back to to his mama? *(BUDDY climbs on SHOWERS' shoulders and they move Downstage to the edge of the stage.)*

SHOWERS: Careful now, pal. You all right?

BUDDY: Yeah. How 'bout you?

SHOWERS: Oh, you're awful heavy! Now watch yourself up there. You got him?

BUDDY: *(As he places the bird in the tree.)* What color's that?

SHOWERS: That's green.

BUDDY: Green? Trees is green. Weeds is green. Grass is green. And birds're blue.

SHOWERS: *(Letting the boy down)* You're awful smart first thing in the mornin'. *(BUDDY lies on the stage floor looking up at the trees.)*

BUDDY: Like to live up there with him. His arms turn to wings and his wings turn to feathers.

SHOWERS: How'd you get down?

BUDDY: He'd just fly down, C. C.

SHOWERS: Well, if you're gonna be barnstormin', you'd best get your wings out.

BUDDY: Like a bird? *(SHOWERS holds onto the boy's arms, slowly lifting his upper body until the boy stands on his toes with his arms extended.)*

SHOWERS: Like a bird.

BUDDY: Is he flyin'?

SHOWERS: Shut your eyes, now.

BUDDY: Is he flyin'?

SHOWERS: If you're willin' to fly, pal, I'm willin' to witness.

BUDDY: Lift him higher.

SHOWERS: Higher?

BUDDY: Lift him way up the sky! Clear up the sky!

SHOWERS: Higher?

BUDDY: Higher! *(BUDDY runs to a high platform.)*

SHOWERS: *(As if calling a great distance.)* **How's the air up there?**

BUDDY: Blue!

SHOWERS: Where's Buddy Layman?

BUDDY: He's flyin'!

SHOWERS: Flyin'!

BUDDY: Flyin' clear up the sky! Way up the sky!

SHOWERS: Have you seen Mr. Lindbergh? Any word from Mr. Lindbergh?

BUDDY: Mr. Who?

SHOWERS: Mr. Lindbergh!

BUDDY: Ain't nobody flyin' but birds.

SHOWERS: Any sign a Buddy Layman?

BUDDY: Who's Buddy Layman?!

SHOWERS: He's a good boy.

BUDDY: *(Pleased)* He is?

SHOWERS: He's a smart boy. I know him.

BUDDY: Have you seen Mr. C. C.?

SHOWERS: Mr. Who?

BUDDY: Mr. C. C.?

SHOWERS: Who's Mr. C. C.?

BUDDY: He's a bird! *(SHOWERS has spread his arms and moves up behind the boy. The distance games with their voices stop.)*

SHOWERS: A bird brain, you mean.

BUDDY: Hey, C. C.? You flyin'?

SHOWERS: Keep your eyes closed.

BUDDY: *(Amazed)* You're flyin'.

SHOWERS: Want a go higher?

BUDDY: He wants to go where you go, C. C.

SHOWERS: I'm stayin' right here with you.

BUDDY: You like it here?

SHOWERS: I like it just fine.

BUDDY: *(Softly)* You like the wind?

SHOWERS: Feels nice . . .

BUDDY: Feels soft . . .

SHOWERS: That's a nice sort a feelin'.

BUDDY: His mama's soft like the wind. Her voice's soft when he's sleepin'.

SHOWERS: That's a dream, my friend.

BUDDY: *(Concerned)* Is angels a dream?

SHOWERS: Buddy.

BUDDY: How come he can't find her?

SHOWERS: Your mama's been gone a long time now.

BUDDY: He wants her so bad.

SHOWERS: I know.

BUDDY: If his arms turn to wings and his wings turn to feathers he could find her in the sky, maybe, C. C. *(The boy moves away from SHOWERS.)* If he's flyin' he could be with his mama.

SHOWERS: Buddy, listen to me . . .

BUDDY: *(Overlapping)* They could fly in the sky, in the wind, in the sun! He could be with his mama! They could fly and they fly and they fly!

SHOWERS: *(Overlapping from the next to last "fly")* Your mama's not here anymore!

BUDDY: He has to find her!

SHOWERS: *(Forceful)* No! You have to remember! She's left you a father and a sister and there's friends here for Buddy! And they want him and need him and love him! And he isn't a bird — he's a boy! You're a boy. You're a son. You're a brother. And you're a friend.

BUDDY: *(Moved)* **And you like him?**

SHOWERS: I like him a lot.

BUDDY: That's somethin', huh?

SHOWERS: You know it is.

BUDDY: Hey C. C.? You know what?

SHOWERS: What?

BUDDY: *(Shakes his hand.)* **You're a good guy.**

SHOWERS: I am, huh? Well, you too!

BUDDY: Buddy is?

SHOWERS: Sure you are.

BUDDY: You know what else he is, C. C.? He's itchin'.

SHOWERS: Still itchin'?

BUDDY: Right there, C. C. Itchin' right there.

SHOWERS: Well, the skin looks a little red yet.

BUDDY: He don't want no more itch-juice.

SHOWERS: You'll never get better if you keep scratchin', Bud.

BUDDY: Well it itches!

SHOWERS: I know — but anytime your legs start to get at you, you say, "I'm gonna save this scratch for another time." *(SHOWERS starts to cross away.)*

BUDDY: Hey, C. C.? When's it gonna be another time?

SHOWERS: After you're better.

BUDDY: Is he better now?

SHOWERS: Nope.

BUDDY: Not yet?

SHOWERS: Not quite.

DOCTOR FAUSTUS

by
CHRISTOPHER MARLOWE

The play is set in Wittenberg, Germany, home of the legendary scholar, Faustus. Having mastered all the legitimate fields of study — philosophy, medicine, law, and theology — Faustus is still not satisfied. He decides to turn his energies to magic. In the present sequence, Scene 3 of Act 1, he conjures up a chief demon, Mephistopheles, and offers Satan his soul in exchange for twenty-four years of Mephistopheles' service. In his Latin incantation, Faustus first addresses his prayer to the gods of Acheron, a river in Hades; after rejecting the three-fold spirit of Jehovah, he appeals to the elements of fire, air, water, and earth and then to Lucifer, Beelzebub, and Demogorgon to make Mephistopheles appear. The word "Dragon" in the midst of this speech is probably a stage direction which indicates the brief appearance of a monster. He next asks why Mephistopheles delays his appearance and then, by appealing to Jehovah, Gehenna (hell), the holy water which he is sprinkling, the sign of the cross which he is making, and his prayers, he commands him to arise. When Mephistopheles appears in the form of a demon, Faustus commands him to go back and reappear in the form of a monk. In the last line of Latin before Mephistopheles appears, Faustus says, "Why don't you return in the guise of a friar, Mephistopheles?"

Christopher Marlowe probably wrote *The Tragical History of the Life and Death of Doctor Faustus* in 1592, the year before his death. The first production of which records survive occurred in 1594.

Many editions of *Doctor Faustus* have been published.

FAUSTUS: Now that the gloomy shadow of the night,
Longing to view Orion's drizzling look,
Leaps from th'Antarctick world unto the sky,
And dims the Welkin with her pitchy breath,
Faustus, begin thine incantations
And try if devils will obey thy hest,
Seeing thou hast prayed and sacrificed to them.
Within this circle is Jehovah's name
Forward and backward anagrammatised:

The abbreviated names of holy saints,
Figures of every adjunct to the heavens,
And characters of signs and evening stars,
By which the spirits are enforced to rise.
Then fear not, Faustus, to be resolute
And try the utmost magic can perform.
(Thunder)
Sint mihi dei acherontis propitii, valeat numen triplex Jehovae,
ignei, areii, aquatani spiritus salvete: orientis princeps
Beelzebub, inferni ardentis monarcha et demigorgon, propitiamus vos,
ut appareat, et surgat Mephistopheles (Dragon) quod tumeraris: per Jehovam, gehennam, et consecratam aquam
quam nunc spargo; signumque crucis quod nunc facio; et per
vota nostra ipse nunc surgat nobis dicatus Mephistopheles.
(Enter a DEVIL.)
I charge thee to return and change thy shape.
Thou art too ugly to attend on me.
Go, and return an old Franciscan friar:
That holy shape becomes a devil best.
(Exit DEVIL.)
I see there's virtue in my heavenly words.
Who would not be proficient in this art?
How pliant is this Mephistopheles!
Full of obedience and humility,
Such is the force of magic and my spells.
Now, Faustus, thou art conjuror laureate:
Thou canst command great Mephistopheles.
Quin redis Mephistopheles fratis imagine.
(Enter MEPHISTOPHELES.)
MEPHISTOPHELES: Now, Faustus, what wouldst thou

have me do?

FAUSTUS: I charge thee wait upon me whilst I live,
To do whatever Faustus shall command,
Be it to make the moon drop from her sphere,
Or the ocean to overwhelm the world.

MEPHISTOPHELES: I am a servant to great Lucifer,
And may not follow thee without his leave.
No more than he commands must we perform.

FAUSTUS: Did not he charge thee to appear to me?

MEPHISTOPHELES: No, I came now hither of mine own
accord.

FAUSTUS: Did not my conjuring speeches raise thee?
Speak.

MEPHISTOPHELES: That was the cause, but yet *per
accidens;*
For when we hear one rack the name of God,
Abjure the Scriptures and his savior Christ,
We fly in hope to get his glorious soul.
Nor will we come unless he use such means
Whereby he is in danger to be damned.
Therefore the shortest cut for conjuring
Is stoutly to abjure all godliness
And pray devoutly to the prince of hell.

FAUSTUS: So Faustus hath already done, and holds this
principle:
There is no chief but only Beelzebub,
To whom Faustus doth dedicate himself.
This word 'damnation' terrifies not me,
For I confound hell in elysium.
My ghost be with the old philosophers.
But leaving these vain trifles of men's souls,
Tell me, what is that Lucifer, thy lord?

MEPHISTOPHELES: Arch-regent and commander of all
spirits.

FAUSTUS: Was not that Lucifer an angel once?

MEPHISTOPHELES: Yes, Faustus, and most dearly loved

of God.

FAUSTUS: How comes it then that he is prince of devils?

MEPHISTOPHELES: Oh, by aspiring pride and insolence,
    For which God threw him from the face of heaven.

FAUSTUS: And what are you that live with Lucifer?

MEPHISTOPHELES: Unhappy spirits that fell with
    Lucifer.
    Conspired against our God with Lucifer,
    And are for ever damned with Lucifer.

FAUSTUS: Where are you damned?

MEPHISTOPHELES: In hell.

FAUSTUS: How comes it then that thou art out of hell?

MEPHISTOPHELES: Why, this is hell, nor am I out of it.
    Think'st thou that I that saw the face of God
    And tasted the eternal joys of heaven,
    Am not tormented with ten thousand hells
    In being deprived of everlasting bliss?
    Oh, Faustus, leave these frivolous demands,
    Which strike a terror to my fainting soul.

FAUSTUS: What, is great Mephistopheles so passionate
    For being deprived of the joys of heaven?
    Learn thou of Faustus manly fortitude,
    And scorn those joys thou never shalt possess.
    Go, bear these tidings to great Lucifer,
    Seeing Faustus hath incurred eternal death
    By desperate thoughts against Jove's deity.
    Say he surrenders up to him his soul,
    So he will spare him four and twenty years,
    Letting him live in all voluptuousness,
    Having thee ever to attend on me,
    To give me whatsoever I shall ask,
    To tell me whatsoever I demand,
    To slay mine enemies and to aid my friends
    And always be obedient to my will.
    Go, and return to mighty Lucifer,
    And meet me in my study at midnight,

And then resolve me of thy master's mind.

MEPHISTOPHELES: I will, Faustus.

(Exit)

FAUSTUS: Had I as many souls as there be stars,
I'd give them all for Mephistopheles.
By him I'll be great emperor of the world,
And make a bridge through the air
To pass the ocean. With a band of men
I'll join the hills that bind the Affrick shore,
And make that country continent to Spain,
And both contributory to my crown.
The Emperor shall not live but by my leave,
Nor any potentate of Germany.
Now that I have obtained what I desired,
I'll live in speculation of this art
Till Mephistopheles return again.

HOW I GOT THAT STORY

by
AMLIN GRAY

This play takes place in a southeast Asian country called Am-Bo Land where the USA is helping the government in its war against guerilla insurgents. The play has only two actors; one plays the Reporter, who is in his late twenties, and the other, a male, plays all the other roles, including Americans and Ambonese, men and women, young people and old. In the present scene from Act 2, titled "Self-Criticism," the Reporter, who has been captured by the guerrillas, is interrogated by one of his captors.

How I Got That Story was first performed by the Milwaukee Repertory Theater on April 12, 1979.

The full text of the play is available in an acting edition from Dramatists Play Service, Inc.; it has also been published by Nelson Doubleday (Garden City, New York) and also in James Reston, Jr., ed. *Coming to Terms: American Plays & the Vietnam War.* New York: Theatre Communications Group, 1985.

(A small, bare hut. The REPORTER is sleeping on the floor. His head is covered by a black hood and his hands are tied behind his back. A GUERRILLA Information Officer comes in carrying a bowl of rice.)

GUERRILLA: **Stand up, please.**

REPORTER: *(Coming awake)* **What?**

GUERRILLA: **Please stand up.**

REPORTER: **It's hard with hands behind the back.**

GUERRILLA: **I will untie them.**

REPORTER: **That's all right. I'll make it.** *(With some* *clumsiness, he gets to his feet.)* **There I am.**

GUERRILLA: I offered to untie your hands.

REPORTER: I'd just as soon you didn't. When you know that you can trust me, then untie my hands. I'd let you take the hood off.

GUERRILLA: *(Takes the hood off.)* **Tell me why you think that we should trust you.**

REPORTER: I'm no threat to you. I've never done you any harm.

GUERRILLA: No harm?

REPORTER: I guess I've wasted your munitions. Part of one of your grenades wound up imbedded in my derriere — my backside.

GUERRILLA: I speak French as well as English. You forget — the French were here before you.

REPORTER: Yes.

GUERRILLA: You told us that you came here as a newsman.

REPORTER: Right.

GUERRILLA: You worked within the system of our enemies and subject to their interests.

REPORTER: Partly subject.

GUERRILLA: Yet you say that you have never done us any harm.

REPORTER: All I found out as a reporter was I'd never find out anything.

GUERRILLA: Do we pardon an enemy sniper if his marksmanship is poor?

REPORTER: Yes, if he's quit the army.

GUERRILLA: Ah, yes. You are not a newsman now.

REPORTER: That's right.

GUERRILLA: What you are?

REPORTER: What am I? *(The GUERRILLA is silent.)* I'm what you see.

GUERRILLA: What do you do?

REPORTER: I live.

GUERRILLA: You live?

REPORTER: That's all.

GUERRILLA: You live in Am-Bo Land.

REPORTER: I'm here right now.

GUERRILLA: Why?

REPORTER: Why? You've got me prisoner.

GUERRILLA: If you were not a prisoner, you would not be here?

REPORTER: No.

GUERRILLA: Where would you be?

REPORTER: By this time, I'd be back in East Dubuque.

GUERRILLA: You were not leaving when we captured you.

REPORTER: I was, though. I was leaving soon.

GUERRILLA: Soon?

REPORTER: Yes.

GUERRILLA: When?

REPORTER: I don't know exactly. Sometime.

GUERRILLA: Sometime.

REPORTER: Yes.

GUERRILLA: You have no right to be here even for a minute. Not to draw one breath.

REPORTER: You have no right to tell me that. I'm here. It's where I am.

GUERRILLA: We are a spectacle to you. A land in turmoil.

REPORTER: I don't have to lie to you. Yes, that attracts me.

GUERRILLA: Yes. You love to see us kill each other.

REPORTER: No. I don't.

GUERRILLA: You said you didn't have to lie.

REPORTER: I'm not. It does — excite me that the stakes are life and death here. It makes everything — intense.

GUERRILLA: The stakes cannot be life and death unless some people die.

REPORTER: That's true. But I don't make them die.

They're dying anyway.

GUERRILLA: You just watch.

REPORTER: That's right.

GUERRILLA: Your standpoint is aesthetic.

REPORTER: Yes, all right, yes.

GUERRILLA: You enjoy our situation here.

REPORTER: I'm filled with pain by things I see.

GUERRILLA: And yet you stay.

REPORTER: I'm here.

GUERRILLA: You are addicted.

REPORTER: Say I am, then! I'm addicted! Yes! I've said it! I'm addicted!

GUERRILLA: Your position in my country is morbid and decadent. It is corrupt, reactionary, and bourgeois. You have no right to live here.

REPORTER: This is where I live. You can't pass judgment.

GUERRILLA: I have not passed judgment. You are useless here. A man must give something in return for the food he eats and the living space he occupies. This is not a moral obligation but a practical necessity in a society where no one is to be exploited.

REPORTER: Am-Bo Land isn't such a society, is it?

GUERRILLA: Not yet.

REPORTER: Well, I'm here right now. If you don't like that then I guess you'll have to kill me.

GUERRILLA: We would kill you as we pick the insects from the skin of a valuable animal.

REPORTER: Go ahead, then. If you're going to kill me, kill me.

GUERRILLA: We are not going to kill you.

REPORTER: Why not?

GUERRILLA: For a reason.

REPORTER: What's the reason?

GUERRILLA: We have told the leadership of TransPan-Global Wire Service when and where to leave one hundred thousand dollars for your ransom.

REPORTER: Ransom? TransPanGlobal?

GUERRILLA: Yes.

REPORTER: But that's no good. I told you, I don't work there anymore.

GUERRILLA: Your former employers have not made the separation public. We have made our offer public. You will not be abandoned in the public view. It would not be good business.

REPORTER: *(Truly frightened for the first time in the scene.)* Wait. You have to think this out. A hundred thousand dollars is too much. It's much too much. You might get ten.

GUERRILLA: We have demanded one hundred.

REPORTER: They won't pay that. Take ten thousand. That's a lot to you.

GUERRILLA: It is. But we have made our offer.

REPORTER: Change it. You're just throwing away money. Tell them ten. They'll never pay a hundred thousand.

GUERRILLA: We never change a bargaining position we have once set down. This is worth much more than ten thousand dollars or a hundred thousand dollars.

REPORTER: Please —

GUERRILLA: Sit down.

REPORTER: *(Obeys; then, quietly.)* Please don't kill me.

GUERRILLA: Do not beg your life from me. The circumstances grant your life. Your employers will pay. You will live.

REPORTER: You sound so sure.

GUERRILLA: If we were not sure we would not waste this food on you. *(He pushes the bowl of rice towards the REPORTER.)*

REPORTER: How soon will I know?

GUERRILLA: Soon. Ten days.

REPORTER: That's not soon.

GUERRILLA: This war has lasted all my life. Ten days

is soon. *(Untying the REPORTER's hands)* **You will be fed on what our soldiers eat. You will think that we are starving you, but these are the rations on which we march toward our inevitable victory. Eat your rice. In three minutes I will tie you again.**

MAN WITH BAGS

by
EUGENE IONESCO

In this play by absurdist playwright Ionesco, a man who is now a citizen of France travels through the country of his birth. His adventures have a dream-like quality about them; events occur without apparent cause. He is harrassed by the authorities for no reason, he encounters people he thought were dead, and he finds that others he thought were alive have died. In Scene 7 of Act 1, presented here, he (the First Man) encounters a guard who introduces him to the Sphinx; his life depends on his getting the right answers to their questions, but there is no basis for deciding which answers are correct. Although three characters appear in the scene, actors may follow the suggestion in the stage directions and have a single actor play both the Young Man and the Sphinx.

This adaptation of *Man with Bags* was first performed in Towson State University's Fine Arts Building, Towson, Maryland, on September 13, 1977.

The play is printed in full in: Eugene Ionesco's *Man with Bags*. Tr. Israel Horovitz and Marie-France Ionesco. New York: Grove Press, 1977.

This scene from *Man with Bags* is reprinted by permission of Grove Press, a division of Wheatland Corporation. Copyright © 1977.

(Male VOICE calls to FIRST MAN from Offstage Right.)

VOICE: Who's out there?

FIRST MAN: *(Turns from audience, moves Upstage Right.)*
   Me! *(YOUNG MAN enters, Stage Right. He holds M-1 rifle trained on FIRST MAN.)*

YOUNG MAN: Hold it there!

FIRST MAN: *(Drops suitcases, raises arms overhead.)* **Hey, c'mon. Nothin' in those but the usual junk . . .**

YOUNG MAN: Password?

FIRST MAN: The password? What password?

YOUNG MAN: If you don't know the password, you're a goner . . .

FIRST MAN: *(False amusement)* **Oh, well, of course . . . the**

password! Wow! What's the matter with my brain, huh? I just keep forgetting everything! Les'see now . . . You're gonna' hav'ta' give me a clue . . . OK? Is the password a phrase or actually just a word? I can't quite remember.

YOUNG MAN: Phrase.

FIRST MAN: *(Screams)* **A fool and his money are soon parted!**

YOUNG MAN: **As quickly as water to a duck's back.** *(Drops rifle down to his side; smiles.)* **Very good.** *(Pauses)* **What's up?**

FIRST MAN: You mean I got it?! The password?

YOUNG MAN: What're'ya' looking for here?

FIRST MAN: Here? Oh! Here! A guide. I'd like a guide.

YOUNG MAN: Girl guide or boy guide? Or a whole troop of both?

FIRST MAN: Cancel the order and send up a prune Danish!

YOUNG MAN: Excuse me?

FIRST MAN: Look, I'd like to hire a guide.

YOUNG MAN: What are you looking for?

FIRST MAN: Out. That's what I'm looking for: out. That's what I want: out. I'd like a guide, OK? I'll pay.

YOUNG MAN: You're gonna' have a hell of a lot of trouble finding a guide around these parts . . . especially for what you want one for . . . Ya' know what I mean? Out is not easy. Not here. *(Pauses)* **Anyway, you haven't finished your quiz.**

FIRST MAN: My what?

YOUNG MAN: Quiz. There's a pop quiz given at this point. Have you met the Sphinx yet?

FIRST MAN: If this is s'pose'ta' be funny, it isn't, ya' know! I mean, I'm not exactly tickled by you, your gun, any of it . . . *(YOUNG MAN exits, Stage Right.)* **Where'ya' goin'? Hey, wait up!** *(From the same point, a SPHINX enters.)*

[N.B. Possible that SPHINX is YOUNG MAN wearing wings and insect-head mask.]

SPHINX: Answer my question and answer it quickly. A true genius keeps what for last?

FIRST MAN: That's a question?

SPHINX: Answer!

FIRST MAN: I don't feel like it. This is ridiculous!

SPHINX: It's your life.

FIRST MAN: My life? I see. What was the question again?

SPHINX: A true genius keeps what for last?

FIRST MAN: The last word . . . for last: the word.

SPHINX: Upper regions of space?

FIRST MAN: . . . Ummm . . . Ether.

SPHINX: Musical ending?

FIRST MAN: Coda.

SPHINX: Tabula-what?

FIRST MAN: Rasa?

SPHINX: Land of Saint Patrick . . . four letters.

FIRST MAN: Eire.

SPHINX: Brainchild.

FIRST MAN: Thank you.

SPHINX: No, that's a question!

FIRST MAN: Whether I am?

SPHINX: Don't answer a question with a question!

FIRST MAN: Gim'me an answer then. I'll give you a question.

SPHINX: Who's the Sphinx here anyway?

FIRST MAN: You are. You are.

SPHINX: Brainchild. Four letters . . .

FIRST MAN: I've got an idea . . .

SPHINX: Idea?

FIRST MAN: Right.

SPHINX: Right!

FIRST MAN: Huh?

SPHINX: Disturb. Four letters.

FIRST MAN: What is it with you and these four-letter words? So far, this play has been clean enough for children!

SPHINX: Hurry! Disturb!

FIRST MAN: Roil. Roil.

SPHINX: That's eight letters!

FIRST MAN: OK. OK. Roil.

SPHINX: Now that's twelve letters!

FIRST MAN: Roil.

SPHINX: Good.

FIRST MAN: This is ridiculous. And that's sixteen letters!

SPHINX: OK, here it is: the penultimate question. A true genius keeps what for last.

FIRST MAN: I told you that already! The last word. OK, I'm in, right? I passed.

SPHINX: Out of the question. Failed! That's precisely the point, ducky. A true genius keeps the last word for last. You didn't. You blew it right off the bat! First thing! *(Pauses)* Rejection! Rejection! Whoo-whoo! *(Makes farting sound)* Uncertifiable! Rejectionable! Fallible! Out of the question! Whoo-whoo! *(Makes farting sound again; exits.)*

FIRST MAN: Hey! *(Turns to audience)* What the hell gives here? Far as I can see, I aced the pop quiz, snowed the exam, head of my class! What the hell is this failure business? *(Pauses)* Not that I care about grades, right? I mean, I didn't *ask* to take the test. It was just there, right? I had to take a *whack* at it, didn't I? You would have, right? I mean, you gotta admit, there wasn't one of you out there who wasn't trying to guess the answers, same as me. *(Smiles)* I should'a've at least gotten, say, a B-plus to A-minus. *At least!*

THE NERD
by
LARRY SHUE

The Nerd takes place in Terre Haute, Indiana, in November in the early 1980s. In this play, Willum, a quiet, pleasant, boring architect, suddenly finds his world turned inside out by the arrival of Rick, a veteran whose life he saved during the Vietnam war. Rick says he has spent his life since the war living with his brother Bob and working as an inspector in a chalk factory. Finally fed up with Rick, Bob gave him all his credit cards and sent him away, so Rick came to visit Willum and moved in. Rick has so disrupted Willum's life that the architect is in danger of losing his commission on a major hotel building and his girl friend, Tansy, as well. Just prior to the following scene, after a particularily embarrassing event with Rick on an airplane, Willum has promised Tansy that he will send Rick away once and for all. As the scene opens, Willum is practicing what he will say to Rick.

The Nerd was first presented by the Milwaukee Repertory Theater in Wisconsin in April 1981.

The full text of the play is available in an acting edition from Dramatists Play Service, Inc.

(WILLUM starts to set up his drawing materials, then starts pacing back and forth in front of the couch, speaking objectively, maturely, to an imaginary Rick.)

WILLUM: **Now, Rick. Rick, sit down.** *(Pause)* **Put down your tambourine. Now, as you know, there's a kind of — chemistry between any two people, which can affect both people in very different ways. Now, just as there's some chemistry in you which allows you**

to like my company — there's some chemistry in me that just always makes me want to scratch your face off. *(Abandoning that)* No, um — *(Trying again — the no-nonsense approach.)* Rick, I'm not going to mince words. It's time for you to leave. We needn't go into all the reasons; let's just say it's something I've thought about and have decided on. Now, I realize that you saved my life. I owe you my life. I acknowledge that. And I realize that I promised — promised in writing — that as long as I was alive, you could come to me for anything, and that you would always have a place that you could — *(Breaking off again)* Oh, God. *(He picks up a large T-square.)* Rick, do you know what this is? This is a crossbow. *(Dispatching the imaginary Rick with an arrow.)* **Thhhkkk!** *(Turning the T-square on himself.)* **Thhhkkk!** *(He drops, slain, to the sofa. Presently he opens his eyes again.)* Oh, me. Oh, well. *(Getting back to work.)* OK. Concentrate. If I just — concentrate. *(WILLUM works, clenching a pencil far back in his teeth like a bit. Momentarily, in comes RICK, hands in pockets, head to one side — in a word, depressed. He sighs. WILLUM works. He sighs again, more loudly. WILLUM looks up grimly, the pencil still clenched in his teeth.)*

RICK: What are you smileen' about? *(WILLUM takes the pencil from his mouth, goes back to work.)* **I'm not smileen'. 'Cause you wanta know why?** *(No answer)* **Huh?** *(No answer)* **You wanta know why I'm not smileen'?** *(No answer)* **Huh?**

WILLUM: *(Stopping work)* **All right. What's the problem?**

RICK: **You really want to know?**

WILLUM: **Sure.**

RICK: **Really?**

WILLUM: **Rick.**

RICK: *(Sighs)* **Well — you know my brother Bob?**

WILLUM: **Brother Bob, yes.**

RICK: I called him up this morneen', and you know what?

WILLUM: What?

RICK: He moved.

WILLUM: He — he moved?

RICK: Yep.

WILLUM: Moved where?

RICK: That was the thing. He didn't leave any forwardeen' address. It was so strange.

WILLUM: *(Hoping he is right)* Well, surely — if he really has moved, surely he'll get in touch.

RICK: I don't know. I hope he at least sends my things.

WILLUM: Your things? What things?

RICK: My clothes? My chemistry set?

WILLUM: Uh —

RICK: My Chihuahua?

WILLUM: Your Chihuahua?

RICK: Yeah. Oh, you should see him. He's really lifelike.

WILLUM: Rick, wait. Where — where would Bob send your things?

RICK: *(Shrugs)* Here, right?

WILLUM: Uh — here?

RICK: This is where I am, right?

WILLUM: Rick —? *(He tries to go on, but can only manage to repeat.)* Rick —?

RICK: *(Giving him his full attention)* What?

WILLUM: Rick — there's something I have to say. *(RICK watches him with his all-purpose expression.)* All right. Here goes. Now — you're here. And I'm here. *(Stalling to think)* Um . . . OK. Are you with me so far?

RICK: I'm a little bit lost.

WILLUM: Rick, all I said was, "You're here and I'm here."

RICK: Oh.

WILLUM: *(Exhales audibly.)* All right. Now — when — when two people are together a lot of the time, they can't help influencing each other, and influencing each other's ability to function. You — are you still with me?

RICK: *(Nods)* You're here and I'm here.

WILLUM: *(Uncertainly)* **Rrright.** *(Should he go back? He decides to press on.)* **So. What we're talking about, really, is personality, isn't it? Uh —** *(Telling a joke on himself)* **I mean, I know there are qualities in me that make it hard for some people to have me around — I'm sloppy, I lose things, I'm always getting lost. Some people aren't able to deal with that; it's not their fault, it's not my fault, it's just — personality. You see what I'm driving at?** *(RICK gives a more-or-less affirmative shrug.)* **OK . . . So, we all have these character traits. So, what if, just out of curiosity —** *(Trying to sound hypothetical)* **what if somebody were to say to you — oh — "Get out of here and don't ever come back" — something like that. I mean, I know it's hard, but if you stood back, do you think you could see what might lead a person to say that to you?**

RICK: Oh, sure.

WILLUM: Really?

RICK: Oh, sure.

WILLUM: Oh, Rick. That's great.

RICK: Sure. Like if he hated me because I believed in God?

WILLUM: Oh, Rick.

RICK: Or believed in God, or — *(Getting into it like a game)* or maybe he hates people 'cause they work in a factory?

WILLUM: *(A quiet moan)* **Ahhh . . .**

RICK: And he hates me because my hands are all rough, and stained with honest chalk? Y'know?

WILLUM: Rick. No. No decent person would hate you for —

RICK: Or, what else? Oh! *(The best yet.)* **How 'bout because I was in the war? And this guy hates people with purple hearts?**

WILLUM: **Oh, God.**

RICK: **What?**

WILLUM: **Nothing. Nothing. All right, just — let me ask you this. What would you say are the main differences between you — and me?**

RICK: *(Shrugs)* **None.**

WILLUM: **None? You mean you and I are — are —?**

RICK: **The same. Sure.** *(WILLUM looks at him a long moment, then picks up his T-square.)*

WILLUM: **Rick, do you know what this is?** *(RICK shrugs. WILLUM gives up both his campaign and his fantasy.)* **It's a T-square. I've got to get back to work.**

RICK: **'Kay. That was fun.**

WILLUM: *(Shakily lighting a cigarette)* **Great.**

RICK: **You smoke cigarettes?**

WILLUM: **Yeah.**

RICK: **Since when?**

WILLUM: **Since the airport.** *(He is searching for something.)*

RICK: **Oh, that reminds me. Hey, I bet you don't think I don't know what you're lookeen' for, right?**

WILLUM: **What?**

RICK: **Right?**

WILLUM: **What?**

RICK: *(Who suddenly is in high spirits)* **Wait, don't even answer that.**

WILLUM: **Answer what?**

RICK: **Or — you wanna guess?**

WILLUM: **Guess *what?***

RICK: **Huh?**

WILLUM: **Guess *what?***

RICK: **I give up.** *(RICK waits expectantly. WILLUM slumps into a chair. It would not surprise us to see him crumble into dust.)* **What? Anything? OK. I got one for *you.***

You know your picture of that hotel?

WILLUM: *(Suddenly alert)* That's what I was looking for.

RICK: I know, 'cause you said you were afraid it was like miseen' sometheen', right?

WILLUM: I may have; Rick, if you've seen that — that's my final color rendering —

RICK: No, I know, so this morneen' I to-o-ook it out, and I he-e-ld it up to the light —

WILLUM: *(Barely audible)* Rick —

RICK: And I loo-o-ooked at it this way awhile, then I looked at it that way, then this way again —

WILLUM: Rick, don't tell me you —

RICK: No, wait. So guess what? You know what I finally realized it needed? So simple. *(He pulls the rendering from beneath the couch.)* **A chimney!** *(Imposed on the roof of a careful watercolor of the Regency is an immense, hideous, black square, boldly executed in some less refined medium — Crayola, perhaps, or laundry marker. A second square, on the opposite side of the roof, has been begun, then cancelled with a large "X". RICK points to the crossed-out mistake.)* **Not this one. That was just a goof.** *(He puts his hand over it.)* **But see?**

WILLUM: Uh . . . Rick . . .?

RICK: I don't know where I got the idea.

WILLUM: Rick —

RICK: God, I guess.

WILLUM: *(Looking closer, hoping that the drawing can somehow be saved.)* **Rick, you — did you put a hole in this?**

RICK: Oh, right, that's why I remembered. Here, look. *(He takes WILLUM's burning cigarette from the ashtray, gets a mouthful of smoke, and blows it slowly through the chimney hole from behind. The effect is made a little surreal by the presence of RICK's eyes, which peer expectantly over the top of the drawing during the demonstration.)* **See?** *(He snorts happily.)* **Y'know, I thought I was a lot of**

things, but I sure never knew I was an architect!

WILLUM: *(Who really doesn't)* **Rick — I — I don't know what to say —**

RICK: **That's OK. But, so — what would I do next, if I were — me?**

WILLUM: *(Clutching a pencil box)* **What?**

RICK: **I mean, you know, in the architect business. Could you like show me the ropes, and introduce me around, and that?**

WILLUM: **Oh —**

RICK: **Or, wait a minute! Hey! We could be partners!** *(The box in WILLUM's hand suddenly shatters, crushed by his clenched fist. He grabs his wrist, pained.)*

WILLUM: **Aah!**

RICK: *(Running to him)* **What happened?**

WILLUM: *(Nursing his hand)* **Nothing, it's —**

RICK: **Hey, you're bleedeen'!** *(Grabbing the wounded hand)* **Lemme look at that.**

WILLUM: **Ow!**

RICK: **You sit there. I know just the thing for that.**

WILLUM: **I'll take care of it.**

RICK: **Sit there. This is my mom's kitchen remedy. You just rub it into the cut.**

WILLUM: **Rick — I'm — don't.**

RICK: **Sit there, now — and don't move. I'll be in here heateen' up the salt!** *(He disappears into the kitchen.)*

SORROWS OF STEPHEN

by
PETER PARNELL

Sorrows of Stephen takes place in New York City. The comedy, which begins with this scene, follows the incurable romantic, Stephen Hurt, through a whole series of love affairs.

Sorrows of Stephen opened at Theatre Cabaret/The Public Theatre in New York City on November 20, 1979.

The full text of the play was published by Nelson Doubleday, Garden City, New York, in 1980. It is also available in an acting edition from Samuel French, Inc.

This excerpt from *Sorrows of Stephen* is reprinted by permission of Peter Parnell. Copyright © 1979.

(STEPHEN HURT, holding open umbrella in one hand, reading "Sorrows of Young Werther" in the other. Carries box of chocolates and bouquet of flowers. Approach of car.)

STEPHEN: *(Reads)* **"Why is it that whatever makes a man happy must later become the source of his misery? I often feel like tearing open my breast when I think of her. I have so much in me, and without her it all comes to nothing . . ."** *(Pause)* **Taxi! Hey taxi! I'm going to be late!** *(He goes back to reading. BUM enters.)*

BUM: **Hey, buddy, could you spare a dime?**

STEPHEN: **What? Yes, I think . . .**

BUM: **Say, don't I know you from someplace?**

STEPHEN: **I don't think . . .**

BUM: **Your face looks familiar.**

STEPHEN: **Does it?**

BUM: **Herman Melville High School, Class of '66?**

STEPHEN: **Yes.**

BUM: **Are you Stephen Hurt?**

STEPHEN: **Oh. Hi!**

BUM: **Hi.**

STEPHEN: **How are you?**

BUM: Fine. You?

STEPHEN: Fine, fine. I'm just waiting for a taxi.

BUM: Really?

STEPHEN: Yes.

BUM: They're tough to get sometimes.

STEPHEN: That's true. *(Pause)* What's your name again?

BUM: Howard Fishbein.

STEPHEN: Howard Fishbein . . .

BUM: We were in Phys. Ed. together. I used to beat you up after class.

STEPHEN: Of course! Howard! It's you! *(They embrace.)* It's good to see you.

BUM: Same here.

STEPHEN: How are things?

BUM: Pretty good.

STEPHEN: That's good.

BUM: You remember those short stories I was writing?

STEPHEN: Yes.

BUM: Well, I sent a few in to some publishers and they expressed some interest. So I'm pleased.

STEPHEN: Good, good.

BUM: It's only a matter of time. How about you?

STEPHEN: Well, I'm working.

BUM: Uh-huh.

STEPHEN: I was in advertising for a while.

BUM: No kidding.

STEPHEN: Creative, you know.

BUM: Yeah.

STEPHEN: "It'll drive you crazy."

BUM: So I've heard.

STEPHEN: No, that was my ad campaign. For Datsun.

BUM: You're kidding. That was yours?

STEPHEN: Yes.

BUM: "It'll drive you crazy."

STEPHEN: It did. I'm in real estate now.

BUM: No kidding.

STEPHEN: Southern exposures my specialty.

BUM: How do you like that?

STEPHEN: It's OK, I guess. You've got to live in order to love, you know.

BUM: Was that one of yours, too? *(Pause)*

STEPHEN: Care for a chocolate, Howard?

BUM: No, thanks.

STEPHEN: Not even a merron glacé?

BUM: I'm off sweets. *(Pause)* New girl friend, huh?

STEPHEN: What makes you say that?

BUM: Or old one, I guess.

STEPHEN: We're very much in love.

BUM: Love is nice.

STEPHEN: Love is everything, Howard. We've been living together for six months.

BUM: How nice for you, Stephen.

STEPHEN: Yes. I think so, too. *(Pause)* Did you ever marry that girl friend of yours? Marissa something?

BUM: Himmelstein.

STEPHEN: Himmelstein. Marissa.

BUM: She ruined me.

STEPHEN: That's a shame.

BUM: Why do you think I walk around with a gun in my pocket?

STEPHEN: A gun?

BUM: *(Takes out gun)* One of these days I'm going to put it to my head.

STEPHEN: Howard, you wouldn't.

BUM: I might, Stephen. I might. *(Pause)*

STEPHEN: Things are bad, huh?

BUM: The worst.

STEPHEN: Believe me, I understand.

BUM: Don't say that, Stephen.

STEPHEN: Why not?

BUM: Because I don't think you do.

STEPHEN: Well . . .

BUM: And don't be patronizing! *(Pause)*

STEPHEN: I'm not. *(Pause)* Say, Howard, about that gun . . .

BUM: Oh, don't worry, Stephen. At the moment, it isn't even loaded.

STEPHEN: It isn't?

BUM: Here. See for yourself. *(Hands STEPHEN gun.)* Yes, Himmelstein didn't make life easy for me. Upped and ran off with another man. Worked in the Dinosaur Room of the Museum of Natural History. Jurassic period. No, it wasn't easy to take.

STEPHEN: We are all victims of the heart, Howard.

BUM: You're telling me.

STEPHEN: Anyone else can know what we know, but our heart alone is our own.

BUM: That's very poetic, Stephen. *(STEPHEN has put gun to forehead.)*

STEPHEN: It's Goethe, Howard. From "The Sorrows of Young Werther." Do you know Goethe?

BUM: Not personally, no. *(Laughs)*

STEPHEN: I've just started reading it. And I think it's very important to remember, at times like this, what Werther said, if I can find it. *(Reads)* ". . . We human beings often complain that there are so few good days and so many bad ones; but if our hearts were always open to enjoy the good, which God gives us every day, then we should also have enough strength to bear the evil, when it comes . . ."

BUM: That's very encouraging, Stephen.

STEPHEN: Is it? I hope it is.

BUM: Hey, aren't you waiting for a cabbie?

STEPHEN: Oh, yes. *(Calls)* Hey, taxi! Hey! *(Screech of brakes)* Well, I'll see you, Howard. *(He shakes BUM's hand.)*

BUM: Be seeing you, Stephen.

STEPHEN: Here's a quarter.

BUM: Thanks, Stephen. You're a real prince.

STEPHEN: See you around! *(STEPHEN exits. Pause. STEPHEN re-enters and hands BUM his umbrella.)* Here. It's really coming down.

BUM: Thanks, Stephen. Thanks.

STEPHEN: See you! *(STEPHEN exits.)*

BUM: Stephen Hurt. *(Pause)* The "Sorrows of Young" who? *(Pause)* Hey, my gun! Hey, mister! Hey, Stephen! He stole my gun! *(Pause)* How do you like that? . . .

VOLPONE

by
BEN JONSON

In this comedy about greed, Volpone, a Venetian gentleman whose name means "fox," has promised his inheritance to whomever will show him the most friendship. Some of those vying for his favor are an old man Corbaccio ("raven"), a lawyer Voltore ("vulture"), and a merchant Corvino ("crow"). Volpone pretends to be on his deathbed in order to spur them on in their efforts to gain his good will. He has a particular letch for Celia, Corvino's chaste wife. In the present dialog from Act 2, Scene 3, Volpone has sent his servant Mosca ("the fly") to trick Corvino into giving Celia to him. Corvino's decision to turn Celia over to Volpone is particularly ironic because immediately prior to Mosca's entrance, he was berating her for standing by the open window where she might be seen by passersby.

Volpone, or The Fox was first performed at London's Globe Theatre in 1606.

Many editions of *Volpone* have been published.

CORVINO: 'Tis Signor Mosca! Let him come in. His
      master's dead! There's yet
      Some good to help the bad. *(Enter MOSCA.)*
      My Mosca, welcome!
      I guess your news.
MOSCA: I fear you cannot, sir.
CORVINO: Is't not his death?
MOSCA: Rather the contrary.
CORVINO: Not his recovery?
MOSCA: Yes, sir.
CORVINO: I am cursed;
      I am bewitched, my crosses meet to vex me!
      How? How? How? How?
MOSCA: Why, sir, with Scoto's oil!
      Corbaccio and Voltore brought of it
      Whilst I was busy in an inner room —
CORVINO: Death! That damned mountebank! But for
      the law

Now, I could kill the rascal; 't cannot be
His oil should have that virtue. Ha' not I
Known him, a common rogue, come fiddling in
To th' *osteria*, with a tumbling whore,
And, when he has done all his forced tricks, been glad
Of a poor spoonful of dead wine, with flies in't?
It cannot be. All his ingredients
Are a sheep's gall, a roasted bitch's marrow,
Some few sod earwigs, pounded caterpillars,
A little capon's grease, and fasting spittle.
I know 'em to a dram.

MOSCA: I know not, sir,
But some on't there they poured into his ears,
Some in his nostrils, and recovered him,
Applying but the fricace!

CORVINO: Pox o' that fricace!

MOSCA: And since, to see the more officious,
And flatt'ring of his health, there they have had,
At extreme fees, the college of physicians
Consulting on him, how they might restore him;
Where one would have a cataplasm of spices,
Another a flayed ape clapped to his breast,
A third would ha' it a dog, a fourth an oil,
With wild cats' skins; at last, they all resolved
That, to preserve him, was no other means
But some young woman must be straight sought out,
Lusty and full of juice, to sleep by him.
And to this service, most unhappily,
And most unwillingly, am I now employed;
Which here I thought to pre-acquaint you with,
For your advice, since it concerns you most,
Because I would not do that thing might cross
Your ends, on whom I have my whole dependence,
   sir.
Yet, if I do it not, they may delate
My slackness to my patron, work me out

Of his opinion; and there all your hopes,
Ventures, or whatsoever, are all frustrate.
I do but tell you, sir. Besides, they are all
Now striving who shall first present him. Therefore —
I could entreat you, briefly, conclude somewhat;
Prevent 'em if you can!

CORVINO: Death to my hopes,
This is my villainous fortune! Best to hire
Some common courtesan.

MOSCA: Ay, I thought on that, sir;
But they are all so subtle, full of art;
And age again doting and flexible,
So as — I cannot tell — we may perchance
Light on a quean may cheat us all.

CORVINO: 'Tis true.

MOSCA: No, no. It must be one that has no tricks, sir,
Some simple thing, a creature made unto it;
Some wench you may command. Ha' you no kinswoman?
God's so' — Think, think, think, think, think, think,
think, sir.
One o' the doctors offered there his daughter.

CORVINO: How!

MOSCA: Yes, Signor Lupo, the physician.

CORVINO: His daughter!

MOSCA: And a virgin, sir. Why, alas,
He knows the state of's body, what it is;
That nought can warm his blood, sir, but a fever;
Nor any incantation raise his spirit —
A long forgetfulness hath seized that part.
Besides, sir, who shall know it? Some one or two —

CORVINO: I pray thee give me leave. *(Walks aside.)* — If
any man
But I had had this luck — The thing in'tself,
I know, is nothing — Wherefore should not I
As well command my blood and my affections
As this dull doctor? In the point of honor,

The cases are all one, of wife and daughter.

MOSCA: *(Aside)* — I hear him coming.

CORVINO: She shall do't. 'Tis done.

> 'Slight! If this doctor, who is not engaged,
> Unless't be for his counsel, which is nothing,
> Offer his daughter, what should I, that am
> So deeply in? I will prevent him. Wretch!
> Covetous wretch! — Mosca, I have determined.

MOSCA: How, sir?

CORVINO: We'll make all sure. The party you wot of
> Shall be mine own wife, Mosca.

MOSCA: Sir, the thing,
> But that I would not seem to counsel you,
> I should have motioned to you at the first;
> And, make your count, you have cut all their throats.
> Why, 'tis directly taking a possession!
> And in his next fit, we may let him go.
> 'Tis but to pull the pillow from his head,
> And he is throttled; 't had been done before,
> But for your scrupulous doubts.

CORVINO: Ay, a plague on't,
> My conscience fools my wit! Well, I'll be brief,
> And so be thou, lest they should be before us.
> Go home, prepare him, tell him with what zeal
> And willingness I do it. Swear it was
> On the first hearing — as thou mayst do, truly —
> Mine own free motion.

MOSCA: Sir, I warrant you,
> I'll so possess him with it, that the rest
> Of his starved clients shall be banished all,
> And only you received. But come not, sir,
> Until I send, for I have something else
> To ripen for your good; you must not know't.

CORVINO: But do not you forget to send now.

MOSCA: Fear not. *(Exit.)*

CORVINO: Where are you, wife? My Celia! Wife!

DIALOGS

for Two Women

ALBUM

by
DAVID RIMMER

Album follows the developing relationships between four high-school kids in the mid-1960s. The present scene, titled "In My Room," takes place in Trish's bedroom at night in October, 1963. Just prior to the present sequence, the two girls, both fourteen, have been playing strip poker with two classmates, Boo and Billy. Peggy was getting into the game, but Trish was terrified. When Trish lost again and was about to have to shed her blouse, the two girls ran down the hall and locked themselves in Trish's room. After they pulled on their clothes, Peggy opened the door to yell at the two boys just outside then slammed the door in their faces. Trish starts pacing, and Peggy speaks.

Album was first presented at Cherry Lane Theatre in New York City on October 1, 1980.

The full text of the play was published by Nelson Double-day, Garden City, New York, in 1980. It is also available in an acting edition from Dramatists Play Service, Inc., 440 Park Avenue South, New York, New York 10016.

Reprinted by permission of the playwright, David Rimmer. Copyright © 1981.

PEGGY: Show them — What's the matter?

TRISH: I can't do this —

PEGGY: Well, you're doin' it, so shut up.

TRISH: It felt weird playin' so near my parents' bedroom —

PEGGY: They won't come back —

TRISH: I know —

PEGGY: You gotta do it sometime. You're fourteen years old! You wanna wait till you're an old maid —?

TRISH: No —

PEGGY: Don't you like boys?

TRISH: Yeah —

PEGGY: Whaddaya gonna do, wear a "Keep Off — No Trespassing" sign on you your whole life?

TRISH: *No!* I want them to trespass on me! It isn't that —

PEGGY: *What?*

TRISH: Nothin'. There's just somethin' wrong with me, OK? This room's so small.

PEGGY: Don'tya ever think about boys?

TRISH: *(Exasperated)* I think about them all the time!

PEGGY: OK, there's two of 'em out there right now, so what's the — *(PEGGY leaps from one bed to the other, where TRISH is sitting.)*

TRISH: *(Exploding)* It's not boys like Boo, or Billy, I think about! I don't lie in bed at night and have dreams about them the way I do about Brian — *(Didn't mean to let it slip out)* — Uh-oh.

PEGGY: Brian?

TRISH: Never mind.

PEGGY: Who's Brian?

TRISH: *Shut up!*

PEGGY: Who's Brian?

TRISH: *(Shamed)* Wilson. In the Beach Boys. I have dreams about him.

PEGGY: Brian? The tall one?

TRISH: They're not regular dreams —

PEGGY: I like the blond one, Dennis? The drummer? He's cute —

TRISH: *(Crazy desperate)* *Shut up!* I'm in love with Brian Wilson! Don't you understand? I love him! I have weird thoughts about him! I could never do anything sexy with a regular boy —

PEGGY: Hey, what's wrong with you? Everybody likes the Beach Boys —

TRISH: It's not like everybody! Leave me alone, I wanna go home —

PEGGY: You *are* home —

TRISH: Oh —

PEGGY: Dufus. What's the big deal? Tons of girls like the Beach Boys —

TRISH: It's not like tons of girls! It's not normal, it's not the way other girls feel, I know it —

PEGGY: It is *so* normal —

TRISH: You call this normal? *(She reaches under her bed and takes out an old photograph album.)*

BILLY: *(Bellowing)* — *Hey, girl* —

PEGGY: *Suffer!* — What?

TRISH: It's this picture album we've had in our family a million centuries. My mother passed it down to me the day I entered womanhood. Lookit. That's where I wrote out all the words to "A Thousand Stars in the Sky" by Kathy Young and the Innocents, 'cause it was the first song I ever bought and my mother yelled at me to turn it off after I played it sixty-five times. *(Melodramatic)* That's how I started.

PEGGY: Started what?

TRISH: See those little pictures of my grandma and my grandpa at their wedding? *(Almost in tears)* You can hardly see my grandma's face 'cause I wrote the words to "Surfer Girl" over her. I'm sick. Look. All the words to all the Beach Boys songs, 'cause Brian writes all the songs. Pictures of them, pictures of Brian — *(PEGGY tries to take a closer look, but TRISH yanks the album away.)* — And you should see the dreams I have! Talk about *sick* —

PEGGY: You're not sick.

TRISH: I'm not normal.

PEGGY: Don't say that.

TRISH: I'm not normal.

PEGGY: That's not true.

TRISH: I'm not normal.

PEGGY: *Shut up!* You're normal!

TRISH: If I was normal, I wouldn't go around saying I'm not normal; I'm not normal like that. *(She turns and looks out the window.)* Star light, star bright, first star I see tonight . . .

PEGGY: Earth to Trish, earth to Trish . . .

TRISH: *(Whirls around; rapid-fire)* **Wish I may, wish I might have the wish I wish tonight.**

PEGGY: **You're not normal.**

(Lights fade out on the bedroom, come up on the hall where the boys are finished dressing. TRISH sits in the chair, curled up, withdrawn. PEGGY ignores her, begins writing her name in her notebook a million times.)

THE BEGGAR'S OPERA

by
JOHN GAY

The Beggar's Opera is set in London's underworld, and its characters are thieves, thugs, professional beggars, prostitutes, and policemen. By the third act, the flamboyant highwayman Macheath has married both Polly Peachum and Lucy Lockit, daughter of the police chief. The two women find out about this situation and are immediately at each other's throats. Planning to poison Polly with brandy laced with rats-bane, Lucy invites her to visit at her home, which is attached to the jail. When Polly accepts the invitation, the following scenes unfold.

The Beggar's Opera was first presented at Lincoln's Inn Fields, London, on January 29, 1728.

The full text of the play, with music, has been published by Argonaut Books of Larchmont, New York (1961), and by Baron's Educational Series of Hauppauge, New York (1962).

LUCY: *(As she welcomes POLLY into the room)* **Dear Madam, your servant.** *(Pause. POLLY is peevish.)* **I hope you will pardon my passion, when I was so happy to see you last. I was so overrun with the spleen, that I was perfectly out of myself. And really, when one hath the spleen, everything is to be excused by a friend.**
(She sings the following song to the tune "Now Roger, I'll Tell Thee, Because Thou'rt My Son.")
When a wife's in her pout,
— As she's sometimes, no doubt —
The good husband as meek as a lamb,
Her vapors to still,
First grants her her will,
And the quieting draught is a dram.
Poor man! And the quieting draught is a dram.

LUCY: *(Continued)* **I wish all our quarrels might have so comfortable a reconciliation.**

POLLY: **I have no excuse for my own behavior, Madam,**

but my misfortunes. And really, Madam, I suffer, too, upon your account.

LUCY: But, Miss Polly, in the way of friendship, will you give me leave to propose a glass of cordial to you?

POLLY: Strong waters are apt to give me the headache. I hope, Madam, you will excuse me.

LUCY: Not the greatest lady in the land could have better in her closet for her own private drinking. You seem mighty low in spirits, my dear.

POLLY: I am sorry, Madam, my health will not allow me to accept of your offer. I should not have left you in the rude manner I did when we met last, Madam, had not my papa hauled me away so unexpectedly. I was indeed somewhat provoked, and perhaps might use some expressions that were disrespectful. But really, Madam, the captain treated me with so much contempt and cruelty that I deserved your pity rather than your resentment.

LUCY: But since his escape, no doubt, all matters are made up again. Ah, Polly! Polly! 'Tis I am the unhappy wife; and he loves you as if you were only his mistress.

POLLY: Sure, Madam, you cannot think me so happy as to be the object of your jealousy. A man is always afraid of a woman who loves him too well. So that I must expect to be neglected and avoided.

LUCY: Then our cases, my dear Polly, are exactly alike. Both of us indeed have been too fond.

(They sing to the contemporary popular tune "O Bessy Bell.")

POLLY: A curse attends that woman's love
Who always would be pleasing.

LUCY: The pertness of the billing dove,
Like tickling, is but teasing.

POLLY: What then in love can woman do?

LUCY: If we grow fond, they shun us.

POLLY: And when we fly them, they pursue:

LUCY: But leave us when they've won us.

LUCY: *(Continued)* Love is so very whimsical in both sexes that it is impossible to be lasting, but my heart is particular and contradicts my own observation.

POLLY: But really, Mistress Lucy, by his last behavior, I think I ought to envy you. When I was forced from him, he did not show the least tenderness. But perhaps he hath a heart not capable of it.

(She sings to the tune "Would Fate to Me Belinda Give.")

> Among the men, coquets we find,
> Who court by turns all woman-kind;
> And we grant all their hearts desired,
> When they are flattered and admired.

POLLY: *(Continued)* The coquets of both sexes are self-lovers, and that is a love no other whatever can dispossess. I fear, my dear Lucy, our husband is one of those.

LUCY: Away with these melancholy reflections. Indeed, my dear Polly, we are both of us a cup too low. Let me prevail upon you to accept of my offer.

(She sings to the tune "Come, Sweet Lass.")

> Come, sweet lass,
> Let's banish sorrow
> 'Til tomorrow;
> Come, sweet lass,
> Let's take a chirping glass.
> Wine can clear
> The vapors of despair
> And make us light as air;
> Then drink, and banish care.

LUCY: *(Continued)* I can't bear, child, to see you in such low spirits. And I must persuade you to what I know will do you good. *(Aside)* I shall now soon be even with the hypocritical strumpet. *(She exits to the next room to get the poisoned liquor.)*

POLLY: All this wheedling of Lucy cannot be for nothing. At this time, too, when I know she hates me! The dissembling of a woman is always the forerunner of mischief. By pouring strong waters down my throat, she thinks to pump some secrets out of me. I'll be upon my guard, and won't taste a drop of her liquor, I'm resolved.

LUCY: *(She re-enters with two glasses of brandy.)* **Come, Miss Polly.**

POLLY: Indeed, child, you have given yourself trouble to no purpose. You must, my dear, excuse me.

LUCY: Really, Miss Polly, you are so squeamishly affected about taking a cup of strong waters, as a lady before company. I vow, Polly, I shall take it monstrously ill if you refuse me. Brandy and men — though women love them never so well — are always taken by us with some reluctance — unless 'tis in private. *(She presses one of the glasses into POLLY's hands.)*

POLLY: I protest, Madam, it goes against me. *(Happening to look out the window and seeing Macheath led in shackles to the jail.)* **What do I see! Macheath again in custody! Now every glimmering of happiness is lost.** *(She drops the glass of liquor on the floor and runs from the room.)*

LUCY: Since things are thus, I'm glad the wench hath escaped, for by this event 'tis plain: She was not happy enough to deserve to be poisoned.

Now Roger, I'll Tell Thee, Because Thou'rt My Son

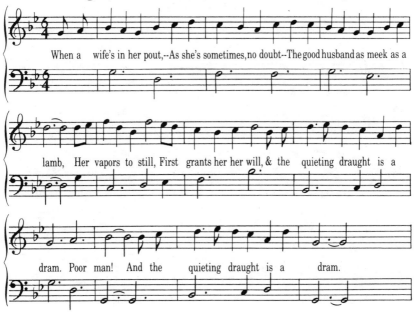

When a wife's in her pout,--As she's sometimes, no doubt--The good husband as meek as a

lamb, Her vapors to still, First grants her her will, & the quieting draught is a

dram. Poor man! And the quieting draught is a dram.

Would Fate to Me Belinda Give

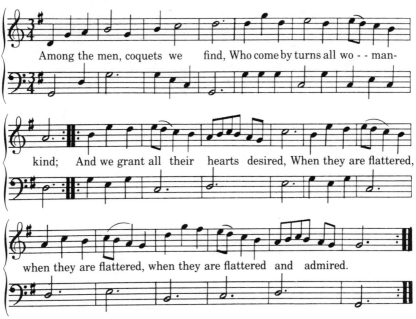

Among the men, coquets we find, Who come by turns all wo - - man-

kind; And we grant all their hearts desired, When they are flattered,

when they are flattered, when they are flattered and admired.

O Bessy Bell

A curse attends that woman's love Who always would be pleasing. The

pertness of the billing dove, Like tickling, is but teasing. What

then in love can woman do? If we grow fond, they shun us. And

when we fly them, they pursue; But leave us when they've won us.

Come, Sweet Lass

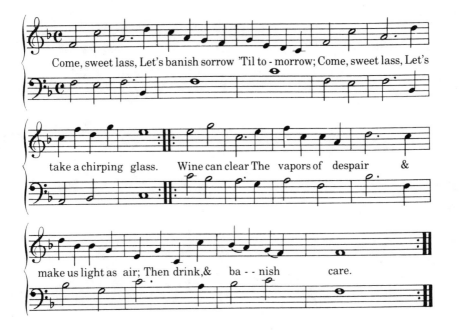

Come, sweet lass, Let's banish sorrow 'Til to - morrow; Come, sweet lass, Let's

take a chirping glass. Wine can clear The vapors of despair &

make us light as air; Then drink,& ba - - nish care.

COURTSHIP

by
HORTON FOOTE

Courtship, a long one-act play from the author's "Orphan Home Cycle," takes place in Vaughn House in Harrison, Texas, in 1915. A dance is in progress in the house, and in the present scene, Elizabeth Vaughn and her younger sister Laura are visiting on the porch. Elizabeth teaches piano and Laura is home on a break from boarding school. Sybil Thomas, about whom the girls are talking, was four years older than Laura. Sybil's wedding had just occurred; however, she was six months pregnant and had spent her pregnancy corsetted in an attempt to hide her condition. As a result, the baby was born dead on her wedding day, and Sybil's own death from hemorrhage has just been reported prior to the following dialog.

A film version of *Courtship,* with its filmscript written by Horton Foote, first appeared on public television.

The full text of the play was published by Grove Press, New York, in 1986.

This scene from *Courtship* is reprinted by permission of Grove Press, a division of Wheatland Corporation. Copyright © 1979, 1986 Horton Foote.

LAURA: Was Sybil Thomas older than you?

ELIZABETH: Yes.

LAURA: She wasn't in your crowd though.

ELIZABETH: Sometimes.

LAURA: Did you like her?

ELIZABETH: She was always jolly and had a very sweet disposition.

LAURA: I thought she was pretty. Didn't you?

ELIZABETH: Yes, I did.

LAURA: I think you're pretty, Elizabeth.

ELIZABETH: Thank you.

LAURA: I love the way you do your hair and the way you dress.

ELIZABETH: Thank you.

LAURA: Do you think I'm going to be pretty?

ELIZABETH: I think you're lovely now.

LAURA: If it wasn't for the scar on my throat.

ELIZABETH: I don't even notice it.

LAURA: I do. I'm very conscious of it.

ELIZABETH: You're lucky to be alive.

LAURA: Yes, I am. I guess they thought I would die. Do you remember it at all when I drank the carbolic acid?

ELIZABETH: Of course I do.

LAURA: I was two, wasn't I?

ELIZABETH: Yes. I remember hearing Mama scream when she discovered it. I remember Mama and Papa both yelling at the nurse for being so careless and letting you near the bottle of acid, and I remember Mama sitting by your bed, night and day nursing you. I remember Papa saying she would kill herself if she didn't get some rest.

LAURA: I try to forget the whole thing and just when I think I have, Mrs. Jordan will say to me, "We didn't expect you to live, honey. We thought for sure we were all going to your funeral." *(Pause)* Do you ever think about dying?

ELIZABETH: Sometimes.

LAURA: I wonder why did the two little girls die and not us? Why are they out in the graveyard and we are here?

ELIZABETH: I don't know.

LAURA: You're not half listening to me. What are you thinking about?

ELIZABETH: I don't know.

LAURA: I bet I know what you're thinking about.

ELIZABETH: What?

LAURA: Horace Robedaux.

ELIZABETH: Maybe. *(Pause)* I'm in love with him.

LAURA: How can you know that?

ELIZABETH: I know.

LAURA: How can you be sure of that?

ELIZABETH: I'm sure.

LAURA: I hope someday I can be sure of something like that.

ELIZABETH: You will be.

LAURA: Be careful though, Elizabeth. You were sure about Syd, but then you changed your mind. You could change your mind again. *(Pause)* The dance music has stopped.

ELIZABETH: It stopped quite a while ago.

LAURA: I wonder why it stopped so early?

ELIZABETH: Maybe they heard about Sybil Thomas.

LAURA: Maybe they did. *(Pause)* Does Horace know how you feel?

ELIZABETH: I don't know.

LAURA: Would you marry him if he asked you?

ELIZABETH: I don't know.

LAURA: You'd have to be engaged first, I suppose. Do you think Mama would let you be engaged to him?

ELIZABETH: I think Mama might, but Papa wouldn't.

LAURA: Do you think you would have to elope to marry him?

ELIZABETH: Yes.

LAURA: Would you?

ELIZABETH: Yes.

LAURA: Even if it meant Mama and Papa never would forgive you?

ELIZABETH: Yes.

LAURA: Don't say that.

ELIZABETH: I mean it.

LAURA: Fifer Ecker's Mama and Papa never forgave her for eloping and her husband deserted her and she died all alone, in New Orleans. What if that happened to you?

ELIZABETH: I don't think it will happen to me. Not if I marry Horace. I don't think Horace would ever desert me. I think we will live together a long time and that we will be very happy all our married life.

LAURA: How can you be sure?

ELIZABETH: Because I am sure.

LAURA: Suppose he doesn't love you and is just infatuated and he meets someone out on the road while he's traveling around that he likes much better than you and he never asks you to marry him? What will you do then?

ELIZABETH: I don't know. I wouldn't know what I would do about that unless it happened. *(Pause)* The other night when I was out riding with Horace he said he was not going to take out any other girls while he was away traveling this time. And I said I would not see any other young men. I said I would write to him at least three times a week, but I asked him not to write me but every ten days or so, because I didn't want Mama and Papa nagging me about it.

LAURA: If you're not seeing anyone else and he's not seeing anyone else, does that mean you're engaged?

ELIZABETH: In a way. *(She reaches into her dress and pulls out a ring that is around a chain. She shows it to LAURA.)* Look here.

LAURA: What's that?

ELIZABETH: It's a ring he gave me. I keep it hidden so Mama and Papa won't ask any questions.

LAURA: Is that an engagement ring?

ELIZABETH: I consider it so.

LAURA: And he must consider it so. I bet that's why he didn't take a date to the dance tonight and why he didn't dance when he got there. Because he thinks you're engaged. Oh, Elizabeth, I think it's terrible we have to deceive and slip around this way. Why can't we be like other girls and have our beaux come to the house and receive presents and go to the dances? I think we should just defy Papa and Mama and tell them right out.

ELIZABETH: I did that with Syd and it does no good. It just meant constant fighting. The boys won't come here because no one wants to be insulted.

LAURA: Of course with Syd it was a good thing they opposed your marrying him, because you didn't really love him.

ELIZABETH: No.

LAURA: Oh, my God! That worries me so. Suppose I think I'm in love with a man and I marry him and it turns out I'm not in love with him.

ELIZABETH: Oh, Laura, you'll go crazy if you always think of the bad things that can happen. I don't think of that.

LAURA: What do you think of?

ELIZABETH: I don't think.

LAURA: I wish to heaven I didn't. Everything bad that happens to a girl I begin to worry it will happen to me. All night I've been worrying. Part of the time I've been worrying that I'd end up an old maid like Aunt Sarah, and part of the time I worry that I'll fall in love with someone like Syd and defy Papa and run off with him and then realize I made a mistake and part of the time I worry . . . *(Pause)* that what happened to Sybil Thomas will happen to me and . . . *(Pause)* could what happened to Sybil Thomas ever happen to you? I don't mean the dying part. I know we all have to die. I mean the other part . . . having a baby before she was married. Do you think she loved Leo? Do you think he loved her? Do you think it was the only time she did? You know . . . *(Pause)* Old common Anna Landry said in the girls' room at school that she did it whenever she wanted to and nothing ever happened to her. And if it did she would get rid of it. How do women do that?

ELIZABETH: Do what?

LAURA: Not have children if they don't want them?

ELIZABETH: I don't know.

LAURA: I guess we'll never know. I don't trust Anna
Landry and I don't know who else to ask. Can you
imagine the expression on Mama's face, or Aunt
Lucy's or Mrs. Cookenboo's if I asked them something
like that? *(Pause)* Anyway, even if I knew I would be
afraid to do something like that before I got married
for fear God would strike me dead. *(Pause)* Aunt
Sarah said that Sybil's baby dying was God's
punishment of her sin. Aunt Lucy said if God
punished sinners that way there would be a lot of
dead babies.

THE FLIGHT OF THE EARLS

by

CHRISTOPHER HUMBLE

The Flight of the Earls takes place at the Earl family home in County Tyrone, Northern Ireland, in September of 1971. Against the continual disapproval of their women, the Earl brothers, Michael and Keith, are deeply involved in the violent Provisional faction of the Irish Republican Army which is trying to take the twelve northern Irish counties away from English rule and unite them with the rest of Ireland. Michael's wife, Brigitte, about thirty, has been trying to get her husband to migrate to America, away from the IRA. Her unmarried sister, Claire Strain, in her twenties, is a leader in a women's group called Women Together whose mission is the union of all Ireland but who aim to accomplish it through nonviolent action and humanitarian deeds. In the first part of the play, Keith Earl unexpectedly shows up at the family home. The women all thought he was still in prison where he had been serving a sentence for having a nail bomb in his possession, but it turns out he has been free and living in another city for months. This news is a particular surprise to Brigitte because Michael has been wheedling her out of the money she was saving to go to America, claiming that he was sending it to Keith to make his prison term more bearable; Brigitte now knows that he's been using her money to support the IRA's activities. In the scene prior to the present dialog, which opens Act 2, Scene 2, Keith has been shot by his mother, Kate. She did this because he was forcibly keeping Brigitte and Claire in the house so that they couldn't alert the Royal Ulster Constabulary to the fact that Michael is about to kill the Prime Minister by blowing up his shirt factory with him inside. Once Keith was neutralized, Brigitte left to call the RUC. Hours later, as the present scene begins, she is just returning from her errand.

The Flight of the Earls was first presented at the Westside Arts Theatre in March 1984. That year the script won two national playwriting awards, one from Theatre Memphis and one from Elmira College.

The complete text of *The Flight of the Earls* is available in an acting edition from Samuel French, Inc.

(It is very early morning. CLAIRE is asleep on the sofa. As the news report fades, BRIGITTE enters through the Up Left door and crosses to hang up her coat. CLAIRE wakes up when BRIGITTE accidentally drops her keys.)

CLAIRE: Brigitte. Where were you? Did you get to a phone?

BRIGITTE: I did. I . . . I . . . wasn't . . . I wasn't able, Claire. I tried . . . I couldn't.

CLAIRE: You didn't . . . You didn't call?

BRIGITTE: I'm sorry, Claire, I couldn't. I tried.

CLAIRE: I asked you. I asked you if you wanted me to go. Do you realize what it is you've done, Brigitte? If that man is killed, we're responsible.

BRIGITTE: I'm sorry . . .

CLAIRE: You're sorry and maybe the Prime Minister dead. I could've gone. I would've called.

BRIGITTE: Well and you should have. It's more to do than you're thinking it is.

CLAIRE: They have got to be stopped, Brigitte. We can't be letting them use a gun each time it suits 'em. If that man is killed . . .

BRIGITTE: Will you stop it, Claire. Listen to yourself. It's no different than Michael standing there talking about the cause and what has to be done.

CLAIRE: It's not the same.

BRIGITTE: It's the same coming from the other side. It's only when I was on my way I started thinking what it was I was being sent to do. Tell the RUC what's happening so maybe they can go there and get my husband for a slow death in Long Kesh prison. And that for Brian Faulkner? I'll tell the truth, Claire Strain. I'd not shed a tear for that man. I love Michael, Claire. He's been good to me.

CLAIRE: Aye. He's good to you when he's not stealing your money or lying to you. Is it "good" he is in the privacy of your bed at night?

BRIGITTE: And that maybe not such a bad kind of goodness. You'd not be interested in that, I know. We're so different, you and me, Claire. I like looking after the men. I'm not meant to be part of the ladies' group.

CLAIRE: You should've told me to go.

BRIGITTE: I didn't know I couldn't. I was angry at being lied to. I wanted to get back ... I'm not strong, Claire ...

CLAIRE: It's too late now, isn't it? I ... I should have gone myself.

BRIGITTE: I'm not strong, Claire.

CLAIRE: Never mind. I'm sorry for asking you to go. *(Pause)* Where've you been?

BRIGITTE: Driving. I've been to St. Joseph's church in Donaghmore. I just drove and ended up there. We were married there.

CLAIRE: Aye. I know.

BRIGITTE: I ... I sat there asking him questions, Claire. One question after another. And I waited quietly for an answer. He used to answer me so quickly. I'd ask ... and then a moment later I'd hear his answer. I was sitting there in the dark and I knew it'd shortly be getting light. I knew I could just ask him all my questions and the answers would fall right down on me just as soon as the sun hit those colored glass windows. So I just sat and waited, Claire. And then ... then the sun came and in came streaming all those shafts of blue and red ... and ... gold ... and I looked for my answers ... in those shafts of light falling on the floor I looked for my answers. But ... there wasn't any. I saw just shafts of colored light ... and no answers there a'tall. So I asked again ... and listened. It's the first time, Claire ... he didn't answer me. Maybe the questions is harder this time.

CLAIRE: You're going to have to make some decisions.

On your own. What will you do ... if ...

BRIGITTE: If he isn't in jail by now? If he isn't dead. I'll stay. And try to get him to leave this place. I can't leave him even though I hate his being ... in the Provisional. I love him too much. There's worse things to live with. He's just a man believing too much in something. He believes in his cause, Claire. I wonder if that's not something good. Maybe it's us is wrong. *(Pause)* How's Keith? Where is he?

CLAIRE: He'll be all right. We've loaded him up with whiskey and put him to bed. It's only a bad surface wound.

BRIGITTE: Were you glad to see him, Claire?

CLAIRE: Aye. I didn't want to be glad. And I didn't know I'd be glad until he walked through that door tonight. I was a lot younger two years ago. I don't know if I loved him. He was there when I needed someone. We had ... a nice time together. Then his damned nail bomb made me realize ...

BRIGITTE: Did you talk about ... the two of you?

CLAIRE: A bit. He's such a boy, Brig. I don't think he'd ever give up his IRA. And I'd never marry into it. So, there's not much to talk about.

BRIGITTE: You've got courage, Claire.

CLAIRE: That's just what I don't have. It's fear I've got. A monstrous great fear of losing a man. A fear of even loving a man. It's you with the courage. Staying on with Michael. Knowing that ... that you might be seeing him only on visiting days if he lands in the kip like so many do.

BRIGITTE: I'm thinking that I might have a child now. Maybe then he'll see we should leave. I'll be damned sure that child doesn't hear stories about the "cause."

CLAIRE: You've wanted a child for so long. Maybe that would help.

THE FOX

by
ALLAN MILLER

The Fox, based on a short novel with the same title by D. H. Lawrence, takes place on an old farm in England in 1918. Jill Banford and Nellie March, both nearing thirty, have purchased the farm and moved there to get away from city life. Jill is frail and delicate, while Nellie is strong and passionate. Their peaceful existence is invaded by Henry Grenfel, a twenty-year-old soldier, handsome and sensual, on leave from World War I. In the end, Henry and Nellie's passion lead to tragedy. In the following dialog from Act 2, Scene 2, Henry has borrowed a gun and gone out at night to hunt down the animal that has been bothering their chickens; the two women have been awaiting his return for a couple of hours.

The Fox was first presented by the Back Alley Theatre in Los Angeles on April 4, 1981.

The full text of the play was published by Nelson Doubleday, Garden City, New York, in 1982. It is also available in an acting edition from Samuel French, Inc.

This excerpt from *The Fox* is reprinted by permission of Allan Miller. Copyright © 1982.

JILL: Well, I can't wait anymore. It's been hours since last the dogs barked . . . ! You've put two extra logs on the fire already. Are you going to stay the night?

NELLIE: No.

JILL: Till when, then?

NELLIE: I haven't tired yet.

JILL: Won't you come up with me anyway? Nellie?

NELLIE: I'll settle you in, but I won't sleep. I can't.

JILL: Why not?

NELLIE: No reason.

JILL: Will you come back down?

NELLIE: Yes, I think so. Why?

JILL: Then I won't go.

NELLIE: Why won't you?

JILL: I don't like to sleep without you there, you know that.

NELLIE: One of these days you'll have to. Forever.

JILL: What do you mean?

NELLIE: When I'm dead.

JILL: I'll go long before you, no fear of that.

NELLIE: Do you know what you are, Jill? You're a faker. With all your aches and all your ailments, you've got a heart that'll beat on till doomsday. You're a sham, that's what you are . . . ! Look, now, if you're really buttered out and you can't even blink your eyes open enough to sit and talk, then I'll set you in your room, fill your bottle, and hum you off to dreamland. All right?

JILL: Are you waiting up for Henry?

NELLIE: Of course not.

JILL: I think you are, Nellie.

NELLIE: I've just told you I'm not.

JILL: If you were, why would you be?

NELLIE: Jill, I'm not. Don't be silly.

JILL: I've seen the way he looks at you, and I've seen the way you look at him.

NELLIE: How?

JILL: It's no good your pretending surprise. I see what I see . . .

NELLIE: You can't see anything with your eyes.

JILL: And I know what I know!

NELLIE: And I'm asking, what?

JILL: You're thinking about going away with him!

NELLIE: Jill, have you gone off your chump?

JILL: I wanted him to stay on because I thought he'd be a bit of fun in the house, but he's begun stamping about the place as if he's half-owner and he's been looking you up and down like a farmer checking stock at a fair.

NELLIE: Jill!

JILL: If you haven't seen him, then I have! He moves to you like a stable hand with a new horse! We came

out here to get away from looks like that, didn't we?
Didn't we?

NELLIE: Yes, we did.

JILL: So if Henry's going to start fiddling around with
that same kind of look then we'll have to get away
from him too, won't we?

NELLIE: Jill —

JILL: Well, I think he's already started! He's not just a
boy, Nellie, he's a grown man. He's got a gun in his
hands and ideas in his head, and he's not just the
sweet thing we imagined. He's got a temper and he's
got a reputation for trouble.

NELLIE: Whatever trouble he's caused . . .

JILL: I'm not talking about his loafing off the work,
although we have yet to see how long he's going to
give us a hand!

NELLIE: Jill, will you hush now?

JILL: I'm talking about his prowling through the
woods! They told me he was out there every night.
Every night, Nellie. Warm or cold, light or dark!

NELLIE: He was fifteen that time.

JILL: But he's got that same kind of look about him
now! Whenever he mentions the woods, or animals,
or the gun, he's got an excitement inside him that
shines through like a beacon. You must be dumb if
you can't see that!

NELLIE: Are you frightened of him, Jill? Is that what
it is?

JILL: Yes!

NELLIE: Well, I'm not!

JILL: I know you aren't, that's what I'm arguing about . . . !

NELLIE: Listen, now . . .

JILL: Ohh, Nellie —

NELLIE: Listen! We've asked him on, and he's said yes,
and he's done nothing yet that I can call a real
bother, and if he's got some great need to be off in

the woods while the rest of us sit by our fires, then more power to him. He's a bigger man for it than we are.

JILL: Why?

NELLIE: The woods aren't the safest place you would name, are they? A gun isn't an easy thing to handle well, is it? Henry was right when he said that those gossipers were jealous of him. They're jealous of us too. Because we're doing what none of them thought we could do alone, and we're doing what they hoped we wouldn't be able to do because that'd prove that we were better than they are! If you're frightened of Henry, then it's for the same reason. You think he's better than you, braver than you. And he is! He can't cook, but he can provide. He can't hang curtains, but he can sturdy a barn. He can't sit, but he can run ... ! Jill, I'm not angry at you, and I'm not trying to slight you. If you're tired now, please let me put you to bed. I won't be long to follow. I promise. Please. Please!

JILL: All right.

NELLIE: I'll heat your bottle now, while you ready up.

JILL: Nellie!

NELLIE: What?

JILL: You won't leave me, though, will you? Will you?

NELLIE: How could I do that? Leaving you would be like leaving half my life. Go on up, Jill. Go on. *(JILL crosses to the stairs with the lamp.)*

THE HAT

by
DAVID MAMET

This short play is presented here in its entirety.

The Hat is also available in David Mamet's *Goldberg Street: Short Plays & Monologues.* New York: Grove Press, 1985.

CUSTOMER: **What do you think?**

SALESWOMAN: **You look wonderful.** *(Pause)*

CUSTOMER: **Do you think so?**

SALESWOMAN: **I do.**

CUSTOMER: **With the veil?**

SALESWOMAN: **I don't know. Let's see. Let's try it on.**

CUSTOMER: **With this coat, though.**

SALESWOMAN: **Yes. Absolutely.** *(Pause)*

CUSTOMER: **I'm going out tomorrow on this interview?**

SALESWOMAN: **Uh-huh.**

CUSTOMER: **No. I don't like the veil. This hat, though, with this coat.** *(SALESWOMAN nods.)* **Yes.**

SALESWOMAN: **I think that's the nicest coat this season.**

CUSTOMER: **Do you think so?**

SALESWOMAN: **Far and away. Far and away.**

CUSTOMER: **All right. I need the hat. This hat, this coat.** *(Pause)* **This bag?** *(Pause)*

SALESWOMAN: **For an interview?**

CUSTOMER: **Yes.**

SALESWOMAN: **I'm going to say "no."**

CUSTOMER: **No. I knew you would say that. No. You're right. All right. The hat, the coat . . . oh, this is going to cost me, I know . . . not these boots, though?**

SALESWOMAN: **No.**

CUSTOMER: **Too casual.**

SALESWOMAN: **Yes.**

CUSTOMER: All right. Boots. Something dark. Black.

SALESWOMAN: . . . You have those ankle boots . . . ?

CUSTOMER: No, no, I want real boots. Dark. Long.

SALESWOMAN: Severe.

CUSTOMER: Very severe . . . all right. I need the boots. *(Pause)* **Pants?**

SALESWOMAN: Or a skirt.

CUSTOMER: I thought pants. Something in dark green. You know? *(Pause)*

SALESWOMAN: Well, you would have to be careful.

CUSTOMER: I know, I know. No, I know I would. And I thought a shawl-neck sweater. Something soft.

SALESWOMAN: Uh-huh.

CUSTOMER: In white. *(Pause)* In off-white. In eggshell.

SALESWOMAN: Good. Sure.

CUSTOMER: This is going to cost me. But I *want* . . . do you know?

SALESWOMAN: Yes.

CUSTOMER: I *want*. When I walk *in* there . . .

SALESWOMAN: Yes.

CUSTOMER: I *want*. *(Pause)* What do you think? Pants?

SALESWOMAN: Well, if you feel comfortable . . .

CUSTOMER: I would, I would. You know why? 'Cause it says something.

SALESWOMAN: Uh-huh.

CUSTOMER: And it holds me in. It makes me stand up. I saw the ones that I want.

SALESWOMAN: Here?

CUSTOMER: Upstairs. Yes. A hundred-twenty dollars. *(Pause)* What do you think on top?

SALESWOMAN: You've got the *sweater* . . .

CUSTOMER: Underneath.

SALESWOMAN: . . . Well . . .

CUSTOMER: Oh. Oh! You know what? I saw it last month. You know, you know, underthings, an undergarment. *(Pause)* One piece, you know, like a

– 228 –

camisole.

SALESWOMAN: A teddy.

CUSTOMER: Yes. Yes. Just a little lace.

SALESWOMAN: That would be nice.

CUSTOMER: Silk. *(Pause)* A teddy. Just a little off. A little flush, what do they call it, beige . . .

SALESWOMAN: Uh-huh.

CUSTOMER: Not really beige. A little blusher. *(Smiles)* I put a little blusher underneath. *(Pause)* Just beneath the lace. Mmm? *(SALESWOMAN nods.)* All right. The slacks, the teddy, not the bag, the boots, the sweater. *(Pause)* This is going to cost five hundred dollars.

SALESWOMAN: No.

CUSTOMER: Yes. With a new bag. Yes. *(Pause)* But it's worth it, right? If I know when I walk in there?

SALESWOMAN: Yes.

CUSTOMER: Look! Look! Oh, look, look what she's got. The clutch bag. Yes. That bag. Yes. Do you think? With this coat.

SALESWOMAN: Yes.

CUSTOMER: 'Cause, 'cause, you know why? You've got it. Under here. *(Clutches imaginary bag under her arm.)* You know? So when you walk in there . . . you know? Just . . . just a small . . . just . . . just the perfect . . . you know? *(Pause)* I have to have that bag. *(Pause; shrugs)* Yes, that bag. The slacks, the teddy, sweater . . . I couldn't get by with these boots, huh?

SALESWOMAN: No.

CUSTOMER: I know. They're great, though.

SALESWOMAN: Yes. They are.

CUSTOMER: *(Sighs)* That bag's got to be two hundred dollars. *(Pause)* How much is the hat?

SALESWOMAN: With or without the veil? *(Pause)*

CUSTOMER: Without.

SALESWOMAN: Fifty-eight dollars.

CUSTOMER: And you're sure that you like it.

SALESWOMAN: You look lovely in it.

CUSTOMER: With this coat.

SALESWOMAN: With that coat. Absolutely.

CUSTOMER: *(Pause)* I think so. *(Pause)* I'll take it. Thank you. Thank you. You've been very . . .

SALESWOMAN: Not at all.

CUSTOMER: No, no. You have. You have been very gracious.

SALESWOMAN: Not at all.

CUSTOMER: Because I want to look nice for tomorrow.

SALESWOMAN: Well, you will.

CUSTOMER: *(Nods)* Yes. Thank you. *(To self)* With this hat.

SALESWOMAN: Anything else?

CUSTOMER: No.

THE IMPORTANCE OF BEING EARNEST

by
OSCAR WILDE

This comedy satirizes the pretensions of Victorian society by depicting the romantic adventures of two young English sophisticates, Algernon Moncrieff and John "Jack" Worthing. Algernon lives in London while Jack divides his time between living in the city and in rural Hertfordshire where he is the guardian of the young Miss Cecily Cardew. Jack keeps his city and country lives strictly separate. He has invented a rakish younger brother named Ernest and periodically excuses himself from his country life by telling Cecily he is going to London to look after Ernest; while in the city, he uses "Ernest" as his name and keeps his country life a secret. Jack is in love with Algernon's cousin, Gwendolen Fairfax, daughter of Lord and Lady Bracknell. The present scene from Act 2 takes place at the Cardew manor house. Algernon has discovered Jack's secret and showed up at the manor house identifying himself as Ernest Worthing. In this guise, he has fallen in love with and proposed to Cecily. The plot thickens when Gwendolen, who earlier accepted Jack's proposal of marriage, also arrives at the manor house. In the following scene, the two women meet for the first time.

The Importance of Being Earnest, A Trivial Comedy for Serious People was first performed at London's St. James Theatre in 1895.

The Importance of Being Earnest has been reprinted many times and its full text is available in many drama anthologies.

CECILY: *(Advancing to meet GWENDOLEN)* **Pray let me introduce myself to you. My name is Cecily Cardew.**

GWENDOLEN: **Cecily Cardew?** *(Moving to her and shaking hands)* **What a very sweet name! Something tells me that we are going to be great friends. I like you already more than I can say. My first impressions of people are never wrong.**

CECILY: **How nice of you to like me so much after we have known each other such a comparatively short time. Pray sit down.**

GWENDOLEN: *(Still standing up)* **I may call you Cecily,**

may I not?

CECILY: With pleasure!

GWENDOLEN: And you will always call me Gwendolen, won't you?

CECILY: If you wish.

GWENDOLEN: Then that is all quite settled, is it not?

CECILY: I hope so. *(A pause. They both sit down together.)*

GWENDOLEN: Perhaps this might be a favorable opportunity for my mentioning who I am. My father is Lord Bracknell. You have never heard of Papa, I suppose?

CECILY: I don't think so.

GWENDOLEN: Outside the family circle, Papa, I am glad to say, is entirely unknown. I think that is quite as it should be. The home seems to me to be the proper sphere for the man. And certainly once a man begins to neglect his domestic duties he becomes painfully effeminate, does he not? And I don't like that. It makes men so very attractive. Cecily, Mamma, whose views on education are remarkabley strict, has brought me up to be extremely shortsighted; it is part of her system; so do you mind my looking at you through my glasses?

CECILY: Oh, not at all, Gwendolen. I am very fond of being looked at.

GWENDOLEN: *(After examining CECILY carefully through a lorgnette)* You are here on a short visit, I suppose.

CECILY: Oh, no, I live here.

GWENDOLEN: *(Severely)* Really? Your mother, no doubt, or some female relative of advanced years, resides here also?

CECILY: Oh, no. I have no mother, nor, in fact, any relations.

GWENDOLEN: Indeed?

CECILY: My dear guardian, with the assistance of Miss Prism, has the arduous task of looking after me.

GWENDOLEN: Your guardian?

CECILY: Yes, I am Mr. Worthing's ward.

GWENDOLEN: Oh! It is strange he never mentioned to me that he had a ward. How secretive of him! He grows more interesting hourly. I am not sure, however, that the news inspires me with feelings of unmixed delight. *(Rising and going to her)* I am very fond of you, Cecily; I have liked you ever since I met you. But I am bound to state that now that I know that you are Mr. Worthing's ward, I cannot help expressing a wish you were — well, just a little older than you seem to be — and not quite so very alluring in appearance. In fact, if I may speak candidly —

CECILY: Pray do! I think that whenever one has anything unpleasant to say, one should always be quite candid.

GWENDOLEN: Well, to speak with perfect candor, Cecily, I wish that you were fully forty-two, and more than usually plain for your age. Ernest has a strong upright nature. He is the very soul of truth and honor. Disloyalty would be as impossible to him as deception. But even men of the noblest possible moral character are extremely susceptible to the influence of the physical charms of others. Modern, no less than Ancient History, supplies us with most painful examples of what I refer to. If it were not so, indeed, History would be quite unreadable.

CECILY: I beg your pardon, Gwendolen, did you say Ernest?

GWENDOLEN: Yes.

CECILY: Oh, but it is not Mr. Ernest Worthing who is my guardian. It is his brother — his elder brother.

GWENDOLEN: *(Sitting down again)* Ernest never mentioned to me that he had a brother.

CECILY: I am sorry to say they have not been on good terms for a long time.

GWENDOLEN: Ah! That accounts for it. And now that I think of it I have never heard any man mention his brother. The subject seems distasteful to most men. Cecily, you have lifted a load from my mind. I was growing almost anxious. It would have been terrible if any cloud had come across a friendship like ours, would it not? Of course you are quite, quite sure that it is not Mr. Ernest Worthing who is your guardian?

CECILY: Quite sure. *(A pause)* In fact, I am going to be his.

GWENDOLEN: *(Enquiringly)* I beg your pardon?

CECILY: *(Rather shy and confidingly)* Dearest Gwendolen, there is no reason why I should make a secret of it to you. Our little county newspaper is sure to chronicle the fact next week. Mr. Ernest Worthing and I are engaged to be married.

GWENDOLEN: *(Quite politely, rising)* My darling Cecily, I think there must be some slight error. Mr. Ernest Worthing is engaged to me. The announcement will appear in the *Morning Post* on Saturday at the latest.

CECILY: *(Very politely, rising)* I am afraid you must be under some misconception. Ernest proposed to me exactly ten minutes ago. *(Shows diary.)*

GWENDOLEN: *(Examines diary through her lorgnette carefully.)* It is certainly very curious, for he asked me to be his wife yesterday afternoon at 5:30. If you would care to verify the incident, pray do so. *(Produces diary of her own.)* I never travel without my diary. One should always have something sensational to read in the train. I am so sorry, dear Cecily, if it is any disappointment to you, but I am afraid I have the prior claim.

CECILY: It would distress me more than I can tell you, dear Gwendolen, if it caused you any mental or physical anguish, but I feel bound to point out that since Ernest proposed to you he clearly has changed his mind.

GWENDOLEN: *(Meditatively)* **If the poor fellow has been entrapped into any foolish promise I shall consider it my duty to rescue him at once, and with a firm hand.**

CECILY: *(Thoughtfully and sadly)* **Whatever unfortunate entanglement my dear boy may have got into, I will never reproach him with it after we are married.**

GWENDOLEN: **Do you allude to me, Miss Cardew, as an entanglement? You are presumptuous. On an occasion of this kind it becomes more than a moral duty to speak one's mind. It becomes a pleasure.**

CECILY: **Do you suggest, Miss Fairfax, that I entrapped Ernest into an engagement? How dare you? This is no time for wearing the shallow mask of manners. When I see a spade I call it a spade.**

GWENDOLEN: *(Satirically)* **I am glad to say that I have never seen a spade. It is obvious that our social spheres have been widely different.**

LOOSE ENDS

by
MICHAEL WELLER

Loose Ends traces the relationship of Paul and Susan from their first meeting on a beach in Bali in 1970 when they are in their early twenties until 1979 when they have been divorced. The present monolog is from Scene 6 which takes place in 1977 in the living room of Paul and Susan's new apartment on Central Park West in New York City. The room is being painted, and the two women are sitting in the middle of the mess drinking wine; Susan is also eating take-out Chinese food. Paul has just left to catch a plane to Los Angeles to close a deal on a feature movie, and Susan is expecting the arrival of her boss, Lawrence, who is helping them redecorate. After Paul's exit, Susan sits back down and leans back, and Selina asks if she's OK.

The original production of *Loose Ends* opened at Arena Stage in Washington, DC, on February 2, 1979.

The full text of the play has been published by New American Library of New York City and by Nelson Doubleday, Inc., of Garden City, New York.

Reprinted from *Loose Ends* from *Five Plays* by Michael Weller. Copyright © 1979, 1980, 1982 by Michael Weller. Reprinted by arrangement with New American Library, a Division of Penguin Books USA Inc., New York, New York.

SELINA: You feeling OK?

SUSAN: Huh? Oh yeah, I'm fine. I guess I had too much wine or something. Maybe it's the monosodium. He looks good, doesn't he?

SELINA: Paul? He looks busy.

SUSAN: I can't wait'll the painters are done here. I'm so sick of camping out in two rooms.

SELINA: It'll be great when it's done. You want to go out on the terrace? We can yell to Paul when he gets in the cab.

SUSAN: I just want to sit for a minute.

SELINA: Maybe you ought to lie down.

SUSAN: No, I'm OK. Lawrence'll be here in a minute. I'll

be all right.

SELINA: You don't look all right.

SUSAN: Excuse me. *(SUSAN rises, starts out. Stops. Breathes deep. Returns. Sits.)* False alarm.

SELINA: Are you pregnant or something?

SUSAN: Yeah.

SELINA: Really?

SUSAN: Really.

SELINA: Paul didn't say anything.

SUSAN: He doesn't know yet. Look, don't say anything, OK? I mean until I tell him.

SELINA: Man, I'd really like to be pregnant right now. I was thinking of just doing it, you know, since it doesn't look like I'm having too much luck finding a guy I can put up with for more than a day or two. Just get someone to, you know, just contribute. Are you happy?

SUSAN: I don't know, that's the whole problem, I just don't know how I feel. We had all these heavy talks when we got back together, you know, should we have a baby, shouldn't we have a baby, and we sort of decided, well, we didn't really decide anything. Just we'd, we wouldn't exactly try but then again we wouldn't exactly not try and then if something happened we'd deal with it.

SELINA: And something happened, huh?

SUSAN: Sure did, and I mean I really can't figure that one out. I've been taking the pill all this time . . . I know we decided to be real loose about the whole thing but I wanted the odds to be heavily on the side of not getting pregnant, at least not yet, but they say that even with the pill a certain number of women . . . and I guess I'm one of them, lucky me. It's so weird because I'm pretty sure I didn't want to get pregnant and that plus the pill should've been enough unless I had a subconscious urge or something, but if I did it was real sub-sub-subconscious, believe me.

SELINA: How come you don't want to tell him?

SUSAN: Oh, I just — it's not that I don't want to tell him. I just want to get comfortable with the idea first so I know how I feel about it. We're the ones that have to do all the work, right?

SELINA: Yeah, I guess.

SUSAN: And then there's this whole other thing of how he's doing, you know, his career and everything. It's like he's finally going after something and it's working out and he's feeling really good about it and that's making everything a lot better between us because there's no competition. I think that's what a lot of it was all about with the baby, you know, I get pregnant and that means I can't work as much so there's less threat, the old story. And I think I'm right because ever since he started doing well, not a word about the baby. Does that make sense?

SELINA: Oh yeah, it makes sense, sure.

SUSAN: So what do you think?

SELINA: About what?

SUSAN: What I said.

SELINA: I don't know. I still don't see why you don't tell him. He's doing well, you're doing well, everything seems to be working out, so what's the problem?

SUSAN: There's no problem.

SELINA: Oh. Then what are we talking about?

SUSAN: I'm just telling you how I feel.

SELINA: Oh. I thought you were asking me something.
   (Pause)

SUSAN: Why do you always take his side?

SELINA: Whose side?

SUSAN: Whenever I try to talk to you about something you always — like I thought you'd understand, I really thought you'd understand about something

– 238 –

like this . . . sisterhood and everything. I mean I have a right to my own thoughts, don't I. It's not so terrible that I don't want to say anything to him until I know for sure how I feel about what my body is going to have to be doing for the next however many months, and then when I know, I'll tell him about it and then it won't get all messy with me getting my feelings all tangled up in the way he feels about it until we don't know who feels what about anything anymore, which is what always seems to happen with us, but whenever I try to talk to you I feel like you think I'm being, I don't know, like you automatically think I'm doing the wrong thing. Well?

SELINA: What are you asking me?

SUSAN: Yeah, you see, like that kind of remark, what's that supposed to mean? Oh shit, Soolie, I'm sorry, I just really, I don't know what to do about this. *(Phone by SUSAN rings. She picks it up.)* Hello? Yeah, he can come up. *(Hangs up.)* I'm thirty-three. If I don't have it now — I'm sorry. But you see what I mean?

SELINA: Oh sure, you have a problem.

SUSAN: To put it mildly.

SELINA: It's OK.

SUSAN: What's OK?

SELINA: You have a problem, that's all. It's OK, you just have a problem.

SUSAN: I'm glad you think so.

SELINA: I don't really think anything, you know? All I think is I'm always in the middle with you two. Paul talks to me, you talk to me, don't you ever talk to each other? I don't know what you should do, it's not my life. I mean I have enough of my own stuff to figure out and I don't go around asking people what I should do because they're my problems and they're not very interesting unless you're me, in which case they're mostly just a pain in the ass. I'd

– 239 –

like to move to New York, for instance. I'd like to
work for Paul. I think I'm probably ready for it
although I think there must be a lot of editors
around as good as me and that makes me wonder
why you want me to move here. Is it because I'm
good at my job or because you like me or because
you and Paul don't know how to deal with each other
and you need me as a middleman?

SUSAN: I didn't know you felt that way.

SELINA: You never asked. And I don't always feel that
way, either.

SUSAN: I think we better straighten this out.

SELINA: OK.

THE MISS FIRECRACKER CONTEST

by
BETH HENLEY

It is late June in a small Mississippi town named Brookhaven, and Carnelle Scott, twenty-four, is preparing to compete in the annual Miss Firecracker Contest. The present scene from the beginning of Act 1 takes place in the living room of Carnelle's deceased aunt. Carnelle has just finished going through her routine — a combination tap-dancing, marching, baton-twirling sequence done to a blaring vocal recording of "The Star-Spangled Banner" and featuring Roman candles and sparklers. She used a wooden spoon for the Roman candle and stainless steel knives as sparklers. She has flaming red hair and wears purple leotards, tights, and tap shoes. While she is thinking over her routine, Popeye Jackson, a seamstress she has hired to design her costume, arrives and the following dialog occurs.

The Miss Firecracker Contest was presented by the Manhattan Theatre Club in New York City on May 1, 1984.

The full text of the play is available in an acting edition from Dramatists Play Service, Inc. and has also been published by Nelson Doubleday of Garden City, New York.

CARNELLE: **Let's see, that was, "And the rocket's red glare —"** *(Then as the imaginary Roman candle goes off)* **Boom! — "The bombs bursting in air" — Boom! — "gave proof" — Boom! — "through the night" — Boom! — "that our flag was" — Boom! — "there" — Boom! Boom! Boom!** *(She goes to mark down the ideas in her notebook.)* **Hmm. I don't know. I think that'll work. I think it will.** *(There is a knock on the door.)* **Coming. Coming. Coming!** *(Before going to the door*

CARNELLE *shakes her head of red hair back and forth, takes a towel from a chair and slings it carelessly around her neck. She begins panting deeply as she goes to open the door for POPEYE JACKSON. POPEYE, twenty-three, is a small, glowing person. She wears a homemade dress with many different-sized pockets and thick glasses with heavy black rims. She does not carry a purse.)* **Oh, hello, Popeye. Come in. Come on in.**

POPEYE: **Thanks.**

CARNELLE: *(Still breathing heavily)* **Wheew! Just make yourself at home. Oh, and please excuse the way I look, but I've been practicing my routine. It's something, I tell you, hard work. But it's coming along. It's coming right along.**

POPEYE: **Good.**

CARNELLE: *(After an awkward moment)* **Well. I guess what I should do is show you the sketches so you'll have some idea of what I want.**

POPEYE: **All right.**

CARNELLE: *(Getting the sketches)* **They're right over here, I believe. Yes, here they are.** *(Turning around)* **What's that thing?**

POPEYE: *(Who has removed a magnifying glass from her pocket)* **It's my magnifying lens.**

CARNELLE: **A magnifying lens? You need that thing to see with?**

POPEYE: **Well, up close I do.**

CARNELLE: **Goodness gracious. Well, here're the sketches. Of course, now, I'm not an artist or anything, so the drawings aren't much.** *(Pause)* **But I think you'll get the general idea.**

POPEYE: *(Looking at the sketches through the lens)* **Oh, that's pretty.**

CARNELLE: *(As if someone has given her a gift)* **You think so?**

POPEYE: **I like them stars.**

CARNELLE: **Well, I wanted to go with something really**

patriotic. Kinda traditional. You know, noble, in a
sense.

POPEYE: And this costume's for a dance contest?

CARNELLE: Well, no, it's not a dance contest; it's for the
Miss Firecracker Contest.

POPEYE: *(In the dark)* Oh.

CARNELLE: The Miss Firecracker Contest? *(POPEYE
shakes her head.)* It's the beauty contest. They have
it in Brookhaven every Fourth of July. It's a
tradition. It's a big event. It's famous. Why,
Representative Louis Pooley's gonna be here this
very year to put the crown on the winner's head.
It's a famous contest.

POPEYE: Well, I guess, I just don't know nothing about it.

CARNELLE: Well, it's odd to me. It's really odd to me.

POPEYE: Course I haven't been here in town but a
short while. Only 'bout three weeks.

CARNELLE: *(Relieved)* Oh! Oh, well, that explains it!
That explains it all!

POPEYE: Yeah.

CARNELLE: Anyway, this outfit is what I'm gonna be
wearing in the talent section of the contest.

POPEYE: Oh.

CARNELLE: What I do's kind of a tap-dance-march-type-
a-thing. It's gonna be done to "The Star-Spangled
Banner." I'm gonna end up spinning these lit-up
sparklers around and around — one in each hand.
(She twirls the imaginary sparklers.)

POPEYE: Gosh!

CARNELLE: And before that Roman candles going off —
(As she shoots off imaginary Roman candles) Boom! Boom!
Boom! Like that — right out over the topa the crowd!

POPEYE: Really?

CARNELLE: Oh, sure.

POPEYE: Boy.

CARNELLE: Well, so you think you'll be able to make

up a pattern following these drawings?

POPEYE: I expect so.

CARNELLE: Well, then . . . the job is yours.

POPEYE: Thank you.

CARNELLE: You're welcome.

POPEYE: Maybe I should go on and get your measurements off you right now if ya don't mind.

CARNELLE: Oh, no, no. Fine. Go ahead. All right.

POPEYE: *(Getting her measuring tape from her pocket)* I just need a few.

CARNELLE: Take all you want. I'll just stand right here. *(She strikes a dramatic pose.)* Just natural. Is this OK with you? This stance right here?

POPEYE: Sure. *(She begins measuring, looking at the measurement through her glass, writing down, then starting a new measurement.)*

CARNELLE: My, I feel like a model or something. Very elegant. Of course, that's exactly what I should be doing. Modeling, that is. People have told me that. They say, "Carnelle, why do you keep slaving away at Slater's Jewelry Shop? You should be up in Memphis working as a model. You really should."

POPEYE: *(Trying to get CARNELLE to relax her tightly tucked in stomach)* You can just relax.

CARNELLE: What? Oh, I'm fine. Just fine.

POPEYE: All right. *(She finishes with the waist measurement, looks at it through the glass, writes it down, then goes on.)*

CARNELLE: You know, you do this very well. Expertly, in fact. Of course, you come highly recommended to me from Miss Celia Lilly. She says you've done some really fine work in her shop. She says you seem really experienced to her.

POPEYE: Well, I'm that for sure. See, I been making clothes practically all my life. Started out when I was four years old.

CARNELLE: Oh, really?

POPEYE: Used to make little outfits for the bullfrogs that lived out around our yard.

CARNELLE: Bullfrogs! Yuk!

POPEYE: They was funny-looking creatures.

CARNELLE: But why didn't you design clothes for your dolls?

POPEYE: We didn't have no dolls.

CARNELLE: Oh, how sad.

POPEYE: Them frogs was OK.

CARNELLE: But what kind of clothes could you design for a frog? They'd look ugly in anything.

POPEYE: Well . . . one thing was a nurse's suit. Oh, and I remember a queen's robe and a cape of leaves. Different things.

CARNELLE: *(With a giggle)* Well, I certainly hope you don't think of me as any bullfrog.

POPEYE: Huh?

CARNELLE: I mean, think I'm ugly like one of those dumb bullfrogs of yours.

POPEYE: Oh, I don't.

CARNELLE: Well, of course, you don't. I was just joking.

POPEYE: Oh.

CARNELLE: *(Suddenly very sad and uncomfortable)* Are you about done?

POPEYE: Mostly. This here's all I need. *(CARNELLE stares forlornly into space as POPEYE measures her head.)* There. Done.

CARNELLE: Well, I've got to stretch a minute. *(She stretches from her waist, then kicks her leg up high.)* There! And, kick! And . . . kick!

POPEYE: You sure do kick high!

CARNELLE: Well, I work at it daily.

POPEYE: I could never kick like that.

CARNELLE: I don't know, maybe you could with practice. Want to try it? Come on and try it. Go ahead! And kick! And kick! And kick! And kick! —

(POPEYE kicks feebly in the air.) **Not bad. Keep on working at it. That's the only way to improve. Listen, I have a snack made up for us in the kitchen. Would you like it now?**

POPEYE: Sure.

CARNELLE: I hope you don't mind, it's just iced tea and saltine crackers.

POPEYE: I love saltines.

CARNELLE: All right then, I'll go get the snack.** *(Exits to the kitchen.)*